About the Author

Aaron Brokenshire is an author, coach and business owner in Waterloo, Ontario, Canada. He is busy enjoying life with his family of four while managing a bustling gym and a coaching practice. He studies health and the attributes that enhance mental toughness. Aaron pursues his love of motocross, jiu-jitsu and travelling in his free time.

HOW GOOD COULD YOU BE?

AARON BROKENSHIRE

HOW GOOD COULD YOU BE?

Vanguard Press

A CIP catalogue record for this title is
available from the British Library.

ISBN 978 1 80016 297 6

*Vanguard Press is an imprint of
Pegasus Elliot MacKenzie Publishers Ltd.*
www.pegasuspublishers.com

First Published in 2023

**Vanguard Press
Sheraton House Castle Park
Cambridge England**

Printed & Bound in Great Britain

Dedication

For those who are struggling and
searching for help.

Disclaimer

This is a story based on true events; some characters' names have been changed to protect their identity. Any resemblance or comparison would be strictly coincidence. This memoir reflects the author's recollection of his experiences; some dialogue has been recreated.

Contents

CHAPTER ONE
Silent Panic

"Courage is resistance to fear,
mastery of fear, not absence of fear."

— *Mark Twain*

Am I going to die here?

The words pounded in my brain, over and over and over, like a subway conductor barking out stops on a one-way trip.

Am I going to die here?

The idea had occurred to me before, of course, but I never imagined it would be like this. No, I was going to live to be one hundred, surrounded by my family, my loving wife, my beautiful kids, grandkids, great-grandkids; a whole clan of little Brokenshires. I would be nice and warm, tucked away in the master bedroom of my comfortable home — slowly being absorbed into a pile of pillows and comforters. Eventually, it would be my time to go, after living a full life, after I'd toured all the continents, seen all there was to see, tasted the most delicious foods, then I could leave this life with no regrets. Not like this, a middle-aged man surrounded by strangers and slumped limply against a padded gymnasium wall. There was still so much left for me to do.

Am I going to die right here?

My thoughts raced, sprinting by me too fast to see, too fast to think. I knew exactly what I should do: calm down, I just had to calm down. Breathe in, then out. Repeat. I just had to calm down, then I could call for help and everything would be okay. I could see Lawson across the gym helping his young protégé with her vaults.

Lawson would notice the sweat on my brow, the whiteness of my face, and he'd call 9-11. The paramedics would arrive, they'd give me a dose of God-knows-what and I'd be good to go. Everything would be fine. Just breathe in and out.

But I couldn't breathe. My lungs were on fire, rasping and wheezing in half-finished gulps as they struggled to keep pace with my throbbing heart. I couldn't calm down, I couldn't inhale, I couldn't even stop to think. No, that's not it at all; I couldn't *stop* thinking. I thought about Angela standing by my grave, tears streaming down her cheeks, a widow at 36. I thought about Gavin and Ava. Who would teach Gavin to play football or screen all of Ava's boyfriends? I thought about my business, I thought about my friends, I thought about all the things I hadn't accomplished, all the things I would never get to do if I... if I...

If I die, right here, in front of all my peers.

If I die. It was a phrase from a foreign language, something familiar but unimaginable, incomprehensible. Yet, like a haunting ritual chant, it echoed in every corner of my skull: *if I die, if I die, if I die, if I die.*

I was paralyzed. The more I tried to think, the more anxiety seized my limbs and froze me in place. Only my heart seemed capable of moving, which it did at a furious pace, squeezing, contracting, tightening, all in one continuous, frenetic pattern. For what seemed like an eternity, I leaned feebly against the wall, seemingly dead on my feet until at last I lurched into a nearby chair and cradled my head in trembling hands.

A thousand images flashed in front of my rapidly deteriorating vision. Images of my parents, my mother's bright, kind eyes, and my father's gruff visage, with the look of concern etched in the lines of his face. It's odd the things you remember in moments like that. I hadn't thought of my father like that in ages.

I'd been so busy, and of course, so had he. Now after years of near silence punctuated only by the occasional brief greeting, to think that this was how it was going to end. I'd never get a chance to show him the kind of man I could become because I was going to die a thousand miles from home slumped in the corner of a cramped gymnasium in fucking Trois-Rivières, Quebec.

Looking back, it's almost funny. Almost.

At the time, I didn't think to laugh. I doubt I could have even if I wanted to. My heart was beating faster than I thought possible. Like a freight train barreling through my ribcage at a hundred miles an hour, it just kept getting faster and faster until I thought it was going to burst from my chest. At least that might have gotten someone's attention.

I held my finger to my neck, but I couldn't keep track of the beats. I could feel the violent throbbing of arteries struggling to push more and more blood to my head, but the pulse was so rapid it felt unreal. Glancing down at my wrist, I saw a number displayed in crisp, bold digits on my brand-new heart rate monitor: 241. I couldn't remember what exactly was considered normal, but Jesus that seemed high: 241 beats per minute. Cut that number in half, I thought, and you'd be getting pretty close to normal for someone doing light exercise. I remembered that a few weeks ago my heart rate had skyrocketed, like it was doing now, for a couple minutes, but my doctor said I'd probably just overexerted myself and that I shouldn't worry. Well, now my heart was working overtime again, and I was pretty goddamned worried.

With each halting gasp that passed my lips, the beat quickened, and I could feel the bulging cluster of veins and arteries course up and down my neck, sapping every ounce of strength in my body until I was sure I couldn't take it any longer. I was completely exhausted. The monster in my chest had sucked every bit of energy from my once-athletic frame. If it would just slow down a little bit, I thought, even the tiniest fraction, then maybe I would have time to think. I just had to wait for the briefest reprieve and then I'd be able to catch my breath. I would be okay.

Then it started beating faster.

The freight train thundered again in my chest, a hundred miles an hour, two hundred, too many to count. I didn't know what was going on, but with every passing minute I could feel my legs getting weaker, my palms sweatier. My heart had raced before, but never like this, never for this long. And all the while the words carved themselves deeper into my overcharged brain: *Am I going to die here?*

Out of the corners of my consciousness, I became dimly aware that Lawson was kneeling at my side. I thought I heard him ask, "Are you okay?" with a note of panic in his normally unflappable voice.

"No," was all I managed in reply.

Before I knew what was happening, I was surrounded by my fellow coaches. Thinking I was having a heart attack, they handed me an Aspirin while trying to calm me down. I crunched the pill, closed my eyes, and focused on just breathing. Nothing worked. My pulse continued to explode, and soon the medical staff were hoisting me onto a gurney. As I lay on my back and watched the speckled tiles of the roof float by, I became acutely aware that they were carrying me towards a waiting ambulance. I knew there were only two places you could end up from there.

Dear God, am I going to die here? The morbid phrase sprung to mind again, more real than before. This was it. The end of the line. The last stop before the subway left town, this time for good. I had to make my final decision: am I going to get off this train or not?

Am I going to die right now or am I going to live? Suddenly an overwhelming feeling washed over me, and I realized it wasn't a choice at all.

I want to live. I'm not done yet. I haven't done everything I want to do. I want to see my kids grow up. I want to see my wife again. I want to see what I'm capable of. Please, just let me live.

*I'm **not** going to die here.*

The days and weeks and months that followed were the most grueling of my life. But I survived. Eventually, I learned I had a condition called supraventricular tachycardia, or SVT for short. This is the story of how I rebuilt my life stronger than ever after my diagnosis, and finally answered the unspoken question that had haunted me my entire life: "how good could you be?"

CHAPTER TWO
An Idyllic Start

Try to enjoy the great festival of life.

— Epictetus

In a moment of crisis, a person's natural response is usually to start asking questions. For me, the questions began as soon as I hit the gym floor.

What's happening to me?
What's wrong with my heart?
What the hell should I do?

I'd been relatively active my entire life. Though I wasn't in the best shape I'd ever been in, I didn't think I should be having heart problems.. I mean, I was a professional gymnastics coach, I shouldn't be getting stretchered out of a meet drenched in sweat and feeling like my heart was going to explode. I'd never had any major health problems before, and now I was wondering if I was going to be carted out of Trois-Rivières in a hearse. Something wasn't right.

Was it my diet? I tried to eat healthily, but I'm only human. I had my cheat days. Maybe I had a few too many. That was a busy time in my life, so I had been known to grab some McDonald's on my way to work to save time. I wasn't obese by any means, but I'd put on some weight. Most guys do when they reach a certain age; a couple of kids and a hectic workload will do that to you. When I was younger, I'd been really fit, 5'11, 170 and muscled. So what if I'd put on 10 or 15 pounds since then? I was still better off than most people my age.

The more I searched for a reason behind my condition, the more I became convinced that it couldn't be entirely physical. Guys like me shouldn't have a heart rate of 240. Sure, my diet probably wasn't the best and I hadn't been exercising as much as I should have been, but there had to be more to it than that. Was I just really stressed out? I'd definitely been pushing myself at work, trying to balance coaching with the responsibilities of owning my own gym and helping raise two young kids. It was a lot to handle. Maybe my body was trying to tell me something. I thought maybe I'd pushed myself too far, that I'd worked too hard.

I'd had a taste of success and I wanted more. I wanted to be the best coach in Canada, I wanted to run a gym that athletes would flock to, I wanted to achieve the kind of financial success that would take care of my family for years to come. It wasn't all about money — I'd left a higher-paying job in real estate to follow my passion and open Revolution Gymnastics with my wife — but I wanted to know that my hard work had paid off.

All the hours of gymnastics training, all the financial planning, I wanted to be undeniably successful.

As I sunk deeper and deeper into my own thoughts, I stumbled on something I hadn't considered in a long time. Why was I so obsessed with success? I had enough money to take care of my family. My business was going well. So why did I always feel the need to push myself further? I couldn't find an answer.

Was I trying to prove myself? To whom? To my father? To the rest of my family? It seemed like I was getting lost in a winding trail of thought, drifting further and further away from the questions I had begun with. I just wanted to find the cause of my heart condition. I didn't want to get dragged into old family history, scarred wounds and distant memories. But it was a long ride to the hospital, and if I wanted to get answers, I had to go back to the beginning.

I was born on a Friday, November 26, 1971, in Hamilton, Ontario at St. Joseph's Hospital. Like I said, back to the beginning. From there, I had what I suppose would qualify as a pretty normal childhood. When I think back to my childhood, I always visualize our old country home.

We lived in a rural area of Waterdown outside of Hamilton. To me, we might as well have been right out in the boonies. Ours was one of the only houses in the area — not many neighbours, no overpriced coffee shops, just trees, fields, rocks, streams, snakes, frogs: all the sorts of things parents nowadays wouldn't let their kids touch with a ten-foot pole.

Things were different back then, for better or worse. My dad was old-school, and he raised my brother and me the only way he knew how. Sometimes that meant teaching us the value of hard work; sometimes it meant letting us make mistakes and learn from them. And I did learn. I learned more from him than I could ever commit to writing.

He taught me how to ride a bike, how to throw a ball, the usual dad stuff, but there were other things too. He taught me what dedication looked like. He was my hero, almost like Al Pacino or Robert DeNiro had walked off the screen of some 1980s movie and stood right in front of me.

Above all, I think he wanted my brother and I to be successful in life. Vague, I know, but that's how he saw the world back then, always in terms of success or failure. Life can be a mean son-of-a-bitch, and if you're not prepared for that, then you're going to be disappointed before you even realize what's going on. If nothing else, I think Dad was trying to make sure I was prepared.

Still, I didn't always see eye-to-eye with my father. In fact, sometimes I didn't even like being around him. There was a darkness that gnawed at him just below the surface, and sometimes, it would come out — or he would let it out. He could be demanding, abrasive, and distant. Other times, he was absent altogether, and when he was around, he was often drinking. There were times when I hated him for that. In the end, though, the lessons he taught me remained etched in my mind long after I'd outgrown that quaint country house.

Growing up in an environment like that can be tough on a kid, I suppose, but don't think for a second that I'm complaining. Out in the country, away from the crowded streets and daily bustle of modern life, we were pretty much allowed to roam free and discover the world around us. One day I might spend an entire morning wandering through the backfields and forests, weaving in and out of the pines and exploring unseen streams and meadows. Another I might spend the afternoon horsing around with my brother or playing in a nearby pond, catching frogs and just being a kid.

I remember waking up with the first shafts of light streaking into the room I shared with my older brother. The smell of toast and sizzling bacon wafting up to our room, and the scuffling sound of my brother Greg climbing down from the top of our bunk beds. Even decades later, all those images remain locked in time, freeze-frames of a life at once familiar and alien. In the back of my mind, those pictures still reside, though I can't seem to put them quite in perfect order.

In one picture, I feel the cool breeze on my face as I ride my bike down the end of our gravel driveway. In another, the glowing warmth of dying embers reddens my cheeks as I curl up with my family around the fire pit in the back end of our property. I have pictures in my mind of the endless fields of potatoes that encircled our house, of the floorboards that creaked when someone was walking on the floor above, of the front door opening and Dad walking in after a long day of work. All of these images lie before me in a haze, sometimes in one order and sometimes in another. The details belong to a distant past, but their combined impression remains. I wouldn't change it for the world.

I had absolutely no fear when I was a kid. Looking back, maybe that wasn't the best thing. I remember one time in particular it just about bit me in the ass. I would have been about six or seven years old, and I had what I thought was a brilliant idea. The night before, my brother and I watched *Mary Poppins* and I was convinced that if I held an umbrella as I jumped, I could float just like in the movie. I was old enough at that point to know the difference between what's real and what's just a movie, but for some reason, I figured this specific feat was absolutely possible. If you held the umbrella straight up it would work like a parachute, breaking my fall and carrying me gently down to the ground. To my juvenile brain, the physics checked out.

So, after school, my brother and I decided to put the theory to the test. We climbed up the TV antenna on the side of our house and scampered up to the roof. Then, I jumped.

"Oh shit!" I remember my brother shouting, as the umbrella popped inside out, "Are you okay?"

Luckily, our house was only a story-and-a-half high and the roof had a bit of overhang, so the only thing I broke was my umbrella.

"I'm fine," I shouted back. With a bruised bottom and battered pride, I got up, dusted off my shorts, and called out, "Race you to the pond!" And just like that, we sprinted off to get into some new trouble. That was the way it was for my early childhood. I was fearless; I was invincible; I was going to conquer the world. I never thought in a million years that I'd be lying on a gurney with my heart racing a mile a minute while I reminisced about the time, I jumped off the roof of my childhood home like a deranged Mary Poppins. Yet here we are.

Soon after my short-lived flight, I started elementary school at Beverly Central Public School, where I passed through the next few years uneventfully. I wish I could say more, but believe it or not, there really wasn't much excitement going on in rural Waterdown in the 1970s. Now, that's not necessarily a bad thing; those boring years were among the most idyllic of my life, but idyllic doesn't make for the most riveting action.

Then, when I was nine years old, my life changed. For years, Dad had been commuting every day to his job in an industrial construction company. Eventually, he became a minority owner for a company named Nicholls-Radtke and Associates in 1977. From there, business picked up quickly, at least in part because he was such a hard worker. Truly a workaholic, he'd clocked seventy hours a week for as long as I could remember. He still does today and he's in his mid-seventies now. I guess his age finally caught up to his hours.

Anyhow, by the time I'd reached the third grade, he was making some serious money, enough that my mom was able to leave her job as a schoolteacher and dedicate herself full-time to raising my brother and me. Around the same time, I received a huge piece of news: I was going to have a sister! With a baby on the way and with Dad's business at Nicholls-Radtke more solid than ever, it reached the point where it just didn't make sense to stay in Waterdown. So, in 1979, we moved to the Hespeler neighborhood of Cambridge.

Moving from the country to the suburbs was a bit of a shock at first, but in short order, I adapted to my new surroundings. I enrolled at Hespeler Public School at the start of the third grade and picked up more or less where I'd left off back at Beverly Central. Throughout my education, I was never the most dedicated student. In the Brokenshire household, that distinction belongs to my brother. He was a genius in school, winning all sorts of class awards and generally making me look like a bit of a slouch by comparison. That was okay with me at the time though, because while I was average in the classroom, I excelled on the mats.

I lived for sports and the thrill of competition. Anything combining those two things was right up my alley. I'd played mostly soccer and minor-league hockey, but the older I got, the more the fire grew inside me and the greater my passion for athletics became. At Hespeler, I started competing on the wrestling and gymnastics teams. It was the latter, however, that would become the centre of my life.

My parents first enrolled me in gymnastics at the start of the third grade, right around when we moved to Hespeler. The decision came as a compromise. Both of my parents agreed that sports were good for me. I was a ball of unbridled energy and they figured if I didn't find somewhere to direct that energy, then who knows what kind of trouble I might get into. Even now, my mom jokes that if I hadn't been so involved in sports I probably would have ended up in prison. So, they agreed I needed an outlet, but they had very different ideas about what that outlet should be.

Dad had been a champion swimmer and water polo player as a young man, so his first thought was to get both my brother and me in the pool. Greg was a pretty good swimmer, but he never had the ultra-competitive personality of an elite athlete. He would try different sports here or there, but nothing stuck. My parents insisted that after we started something, we had to stick with it for at least a year before we quit. He wouldn't complain or anything like that. He just didn't have a passion for athletics the same way I did. Unfortunately for my father, I was scared to death of the deep end, so swimming was out of the question.

Like my dad, Mom had an athletic background. She had been a dancer and trained at the National Ballet, and at first, she wanted to put Greg and I into dance classes, but Dad was having none of it.

"There's no way my sons will take dance lessons," he said.

"Why not?"

"They're gonna get the shit kicked out of them in school, that's why!" he replied, and that was the end of that.

As a compromise, Mom proposed gymnastics. That was something Dad could at least work with, so mom signed my brother and me up. After the agreed-upon waiting period of one year, Greg dropped out, but I was hooked.

Gymnastics offered me an opportunity to channel my energy, athleticism, and competitiveness constructively. Plus, I was good. By the end of the school year, I was competing in events. By the time I had reached the fifth grade, I was training five days a week, and by the sixth grade, I had placed in the Ontario Championships. I started out training in smaller venues, beginning with the Cambridge Kips in their training centres at local Cambridge secondary schools, all while growing bigger, stronger, and better. Finally, we heard that a new national training centre was being opened up in Burlington. This would be a step up and a chance for me to train at a whole different level.

Almost every day my coach would drive me forty-five minutes each way to train. He had a son, Mark, who was just a bit younger than I was, and who was also competing in gymnastics. We trained hard, dreaming of the days when we would be competing in the National Championships or even the Olympics. I idolized Kurt Thomas, the great American gymnast, and I drove myself every day to reach those heights. We were at a national training centre. They had the best coaches and the best prospects.

We were sure that someday we'd join their ranks.

Along the way, I faced challenges, most of them social. I actually enjoyed school a lot, not for the academics per se but for the social aspect. When we lived in Waterdown, there weren't a lot of kids around, so pretty much the only time I got to see my friends was during the school day. Then, when we moved to Hespeler, I was introduced to a whole new social scene. Suddenly, there weren't a handful of kids my age, but instead, there were dozens. Instead of being a single family surrounded by farms, we were a family surrounded by other families. During that time, I had made several close friends, most of whom I keep in contact with today. My improved social life, however, sometimes came into conflict with my gymnastic aspirations.

"My friends are going to the movies," or, "Steve is throwing a birthday party," or, "Everyone is watching the Buffalo Bills game," I'd say. "Why do I have to go

27

to gymnastics?" They were the standard sort of complaints most parents, especially ones involved in sports, are used to hearing, and my mom did a good job of mitigating my concerns.

Sure, I wasn't able to do certain things or hang out with my friends whenever I wanted to, but I was passionate about gymnastics. With passion comes certain sacrifices; my father had taught me that lesson years ago. All told, I managed a relatively healthy balance between gymnastics, school, friends, and all other things going on in my life.

In the end, though, my gymnastics career reached an inevitable breaking point. By the time I had reached the tenth grade, I knew it was time to call it quits. I had reached the national level competition, but I hadn't quite been able to achieve everything I had hoped: I wasn't a junior Olympian, I wasn't on the National team, I was just a very good young gymnast. In order to reach the next level, I knew I had to devote my life fully to the sport, and I wasn't ready for that level of commitment. The final straw came when I injured my shoulder doing a high bar routine at the Ontario Championships. I was fifteen years old, just about the age when you have to make the decision whether or not you're serious about a future in gymnastics, and I decided that I'd done as much as I could with the sport. In a way, I was relieved that I'd been injured. It was never going to be an easy decision to give up

28

gymnastics, but I was convinced it was the right thing to do at the time.

Meanwhile, I had fostered other interests in addition to sports while I was in high school. In particular, I discovered a love for business. For as long as I can remember, I've had an interest in money, in buying and selling, that sort of thing. One of the traditions we had in my family was our annual trips to a vacation home in Florida. I remember one time when I was really young — I mean, way too young to be doing things like this — I realized that you could buy fireworks in the United States which you couldn't buy in Canada. Naturally, I bought bricks upon bricks of the cheapest fireworks I could find, and when we got back home, I divided them up in little paper bags and sold them for a profit to kids at my school.

I engaged in lots of similar entrepreneurial enterprises as I got older, but probably my most profitable came when I decided to buy a husky puppy. That might sound a bit preposterous but hear me out. At that time, my coach owned a beautiful husky that he bred. I saw them whenever I'd go to Mark's house to play, and eventually, I convinced my parents that we had to buy one of the puppies. One day, I was talking to one of my teachers and he mentioned that he raced in dog sled competitions. Of course, being the sort of person, whose ears perk up whenever he hears about any sort of athletic competition, I was intrigued.

"I didn't know they did those sorts of things in Ontario," I said.

"Ya, sure they do," he said. "They're not as common as they are up North, but there are a few races around here. You can train the dogs during the summer on carts, then race them during the winter."

As soon as I got home, I begged Dad to let me take my dog to one of those races. He did, and I spent the rest of the summer training our husky, Chimo, for the Ontario Sled Dog Racing Championships. When winter rolled around, I entered the races and ended up winning the overall title for the "One-dog – One-mile" category, the youngest to ever do it at 13 competing against adults. I was ecstatic, so I decided to try the "Three dog – Three-mile" category the next year. I bought two more dogs from a local racer who lived out in the country and ended up competing again the next year in the three-dog race, though I never won in that category.

Eventually, I decided to sell the two extra dogs, but not before the gentleman out in the country asked if I would like to breed one. I figured I had nothing to lose, so I said yes. She had nine puppies total; the breeder kept one puppy as payment, and the rest I took home with me. I had posted an ad in the paper, *Husky puppies for sale: $500 including the date they would be ready. I took calls and discussed holding puppies of certain descriptions for people.* The morning of, I had people knocking on our front door asking to see the puppies.

I was still thirteen at the time, and I didn't think to mention much of this to my parents who were also not paying close enough attention to what I did say.

"Aaron," Dad said, stomping as he clambered downstairs to answer the door for a third time, "what the hell is going on?"

"Oh, I'm selling my litter of puppies," I said.

"And when were you going to tell us about this plan?" my mom asked, "And how did these people find our house? And how much are you selling them for? And have they been vaccinated?"

Then, no word of a lie, I responded, "Sorry, I'm kind of busy right now Mom, can we talk about this later?" and went on showing the strangers down to our basement to check out the puppies.

Later, once all eight had been sold, my parents called me into the dining room.

"Aaron, you can't keep that money," Dad said.

"But it's my money," I said. "I bred the puppies, I printed the ad, and I sold them. It's my money."

Dad sat for a long time stroking his chin. Several times it looked like either he or my mother were going to say something, but in the end, they remained silent. I got to keep the four thousand dollars, and I think my parents realized then that there was something a bit different about this kid standing in front of them, pockets bulging with cash.

While I was rapidly discovering the wonders of the free market economy, I was also experimenting with different sports to fill the void left by my exit from gymnastics. For a couple years I experimented with martial arts, which I've kept up with on and off ever since. Later on, as an adult, I became proficient in Tae Kwon Do and Jiu-Jitsu. In high school, I focused on kickboxing.

My favourite sport at that time, though, was football, which I played during grades eleven and twelve in high school. At first, the two sports seem like they have nothing in common: gymnastics, with its emphasis on precision and flexibility, football with its raw, explosive power. Upon closer inspection, however, they are more similar than most people would think. Both sports require incredible physicality and, in their own ways, a harnessed aggression. I was the free safety on my team, and during blitzes, I felt the same steely focus and rush of adrenaline as when I was holding an iron cross or landing the perfect vault.

I had the same passion for football that I had for gymnastics.

The problem was my body. *If I were just a little bigger*, I remember thinking, *if I were just a few inches taller, a few pounds heavier, then maybe I'd have a shot at the college level.* I used to play the words over and over in my mind. "If only I was a little bit bigger." I wasn't ready then to accept my limitations. I blamed myself for not starting earlier, for not training harder. I was frustrated with my own failures and with the circumstances which seemed to unfairly place my dreams just beyond my reach. No amount of wishing would make it so. In the end, I figured I was just too small to compete in college, so after my final year of high school, I stopped playing altogether.

The other sport which helped fill the void in my life was wrestling. Unlike football, I found that I had the perfect dimensions for wrestling. Years of gymnastics training had left my body muscular and flexible with wiry strength, perfectly suited for grappling. Coupled with my experience in combat sports developed through kickboxing and my natural aggressiveness, I was a beast on the mats. I had already won the county championships in the 36-kilogram-and-under division when I was in the sixth grade, but during high school, I was able to devote myself much more to the sport, especially after I stopped doing gymnastics.

I began thinking I had a serious future in wrestling. By the beginning of high school, I was already dominating most of my opponents, and I thought I had the potential to go even further. Then, during a high school gym class, the PE teacher had us run some routine laps of the track. We were doing a fairly standard distance run, just two times around the four-hundred-meter track. I'd done runs like that before without any problems, but this time something was different. I was completely out of breath almost from the moment we started. It was as if I'd been through an entire workout before the run began, sapping me of all my energy. I couldn't understand what had happened to me.

After the run, my teacher had each of us check our heart rates. Normally to do that you would count your heart rate for twenty seconds and then multiply that number by three. Somewhere around 120 would have been normal for a kid my age. I put my finger to my neck, but the pulse was almost too high to count.

"You must have pushed yourself too hard during the run," my teacher said. "Take a breather, Aaron."

After a couple of minutes, I felt fine, so I continued on with my regular sports. Whatever had happened, it was gone now.

The next time I noticed anything odd was at a dual wrestling meet against a rival high school. I was the defending champion in my weight class and I was feeling stronger than ever. I had trained day in and day out for these matches and I was ready to show that I was capable of an even higher standard of competition. After breezing through my first two opponents, I faced off in the quarter-final against one of the same athletes I'd wrestled the previous year. It had been a tough fight then, but one that I eventually won. This time, I was more prepared. I was bigger, I was stronger, and I was confident. Mentally, I was prepared for anything. Once I stepped onto the mat, I would be aggression incarnate, a flurry of muscle ready to hurtle anyone who got in my way onto their back and keep them there.

That was the mentality I needed to have to succeed.

Sizing up my opponent as I stepped onto the mat, I developed a game plan. He was tall, taller than me. He would use his longer reach to initiate contact, trying to stay to the outside while establishing an advantageous grip. Once he achieved a position he liked, he would set his feet and push off with his lower body, driving me to the ground and scoring a takedown. I wouldn't let him do any of that. I was going to bulldoze him. No matter what angle he tried, no matter how much he had trained for this moment, whatever he was planning wouldn't work. I was going to devour him.

The referee signaled for us to get into our positions. I got into a low, stable position. He did the same. As the ref barked, "Wrestle!" the muscles in my legs tightened and I lurched forward like a caged animal. Pushing past his pawing hands, I lunged straight for his right knee, pulling him down to the mat and thrusting my shoulders into his hip. With one arm wrapped around his thigh and the other his waist, I tried to adjust my grip and hold on to my superior position. I knew he would struggle, trying to reverse the hold and regain his footing, but I wasn't going to let him. I was in a dominant position. I had him exactly where I wanted him. I had this match locked down, right up until I didn't.

At first, it was subtle, almost undetectable. I powered on, but it wouldn't go away, this tightness in the base of my neck. I could feel my hold on my opponent's leg slipping. My left arm was struggling to contain his bucking knee. If I didn't readjust, he'd push off the mat and twist around my body, slipping through my grasp and pinning me beneath his chest. But there was still time to stop his movement; I just had to re-establish my grip, push with my left to match the strength of his struggle. Leaning on him with all my might, I gripped, I pushed, but to no avail. He was too strong. No, I was too weak. Now I could feel the tight sensation in my neck spreading from the base of my throat all the way to the bottom of my ears. My opponent swung around my arms, dodging past any feeble offensive maneuver I might muster, and disappeared behind my line of sight. Before I had time to crane my neck, I felt his arms like iron clamping onto my legs, pulling me to the mat and freezing me in place. As I lay prone, unable to move my tired arms more than a wiggle, my mind raced to try to understand what just happened. I was in a perfect position, cruising my way to a victory, but I couldn't hold on. I fatigued, and my opponent took advantage.

The whistle sounded, signaling the end of the round. I walked to my side of the mat with feet like lead. Just standing during the break between rounds seemed like an impossible task, and when I put my fingers to my neck, the arteries stood out like raging rivers overflowing their bounds. I had to recuperate; the next round would be starting any second now and I was exhausted. My heart was beating furiously now, a feeling I would grow to know all too well.

I lost the match. By a wide margin. The same opponent I had defeated just a year ago destroyed me in only a few minutes, and all explanations were futile. My endurance, which had never been an issue before, now seemed better suited to an asthmatic school kid than the former county champion. It didn't make any sense. My brother was a good middle-distance runner, and we shared the same genes. None of it made any sense to me at the time.

I'd thought I was going to conquer the world. I thought that I was invincible. I was an Olympian in waiting. Well, at that particular moment, I didn't feel like it. I was just really damn tired. Lying down on the cold gym floor after the match, the dreams of my youth seemed like shadows withering beneath the heat of a brilliant sun.

Stop drifting…Sprint to the finish. Write off your hopes, and if your well-being matters to you, be your own savior while you can.

—*Marcus Aurelius*

CHAPTER THREE
Finding My Way

How long are you going to wait before you demand the best for yourself?

— Epictetus

After high school, I stopped playing sports competitively. No matter the sport — whether gymnastics, football, wrestling, you name it — I found I didn't have the energy to go full out the way I wanted to. I was frustrated. Not only were my dreams of competing at the college level slipping through my fingers, but I was even struggling to do things that had seemed so easy in years prior. For the first time in my life, I felt like I was moving backwards. In wrestling, I was getting trounced by guys I'd beaten before. In gymnastics, I was struggling to pull off routines I used to nail every time in practice.

For years, athletics had been a massive part of my life. Being unable to compete at the level I knew I was capable of felt like being forced into early retirement, and what made it worse was I had no idea why any of this was happening. I had an inkling that something was wrong with my cardio fitness, but I couldn't understand why.

Every once and a while I would feel short of breath or sense that familiar pulsing in my neck, but so what? I was still able to function in my daily life.

"Maybe my body just isn't cut out for the highest tier of athletics," I'd say to myself. "I guess I won't make it as a professional athlete. Most people don't. It's not the end of the world."

I had other interests, other skills. I put the world of sports to the side, and I didn't think much about my odd, racing heart for many, many years — not until I was forty-three years old. Not until I bought a brand-new heart rate monitor, just a few months before big gymnastics meet in Trois-Rivières.

Since my career in athletics hadn't turned out the way I'd planned it, I was now free to devote all of my time and effort to my other passion: building wealth. Not as romantic a profession, I admit, but there was something about the business world that had always appealed to me. Even as a young kid, whenever I was asked what my dream job would be, I would answer without hesitation: Business Magnate. My parents used to laugh when I said that, and who can blame them? It must have been a comical sight, me planning my entrepreneurial empire in between recess and show-and-tell. Still, they quickly learned how serious I was.

In many ways, I was attracted to business for the same reasons as I was to sports. Buying and selling, owning and negotiating, seeing potential where others couldn't and making a profit. Those were the sorts of things that fed the fire of my competitive spirit. Those small pleasures were what motivated me during my days as a capitalistic little dog breeder and small-time fireworks distributor. Now I was ready for business on a grander scale.

My first instinct was to work my way up to a management position, and eventually an ownership one, in the hospitality industry. Resorts and hotels had fascinated me ever since our family started to annually visit a vacation home in Pompano Beach, Florida when I was eight years old. Every winter from then until I left for college we would fly down and spend two weeks in paradise. Well, as close to paradise as an eight-year-old boy could imagine. Our property was just north of Fort Lauderdale in a fairly wealthy neighborhood, and every day we would see Porsches, Mercedes, yachts and fabulous homes, all glistening in the golden Florida sunlight and crisp ocean breeze.

I grew up in an upper-middle-class environment. We never hurt for money, especially after Dad's business took off, but this was a whole different world. This was the life of multi-million-dollar yachts and upscale ocean-side marinas. And there we were, standing on the border of that mysterious country, looking up the mountainside at the seemingly unattainable heights above and filling our dreams with visions of what our futures might hold.

He drilled into our heads, mine and my brother's, the value of hard work and scrupulous finances. By showing us the sort of lives we might someday have if we kept our noses to the grindstone, Dad tried to instill in us a goal worth striving towards.

Looking back from where I am now, that sounds like an extremely materialistic worldview. I suppose in many ways, it was. Dad cared a lot about financial security, and to a large extent, that attitude transferred over to me. I wanted to make enough money to support myself and (way, way down the line) a family like he did.

More than support, I wanted to be able to provide the sort of childhood that I'd been fortunate enough to experience. Don't think for a minute I don't appreciate how idyllic my childhood was. I was blessed to be born in a wonderful country like Canada, to have two loving parents, to never want for money or opportunities, to be able to participate in whatever sports I wanted to, to live in a beautiful house, and yes, to spend a few weeks each year vacationing in Pompano Beach admiring the yachts.

To achieve that kind of success, though, I needed a job. Ideally, one I'd be good at. But what was I good at? For most of my life, I'd been focused more on sports than on school. I hadn't stopped to consider what I might do after high school. College, university, career, those were things I could figure out later. Well, later comes quicker than you'd think.

At my wits' end, I decided to get some professional advice. I'm naturally a stubborn person — if you need confirmation, just talk to my wife. Normally I like to tackle my problems head-on, by myself. That mentality served me well in gymnastics, where I could just practice my vault again and again until I nailed it. But when it came to self-analysis, my brute force approach wasn't helping one bit. I was like a charging bull, always rushing forward without pausing to consider why. It would take a lot of time and a terrifyingly close call on an operating table before I'd be ready to focus on my thoughts productively.

For now, I needed help.

"What should I do?" I asked my high school guidance counselor one day after school.

"Well, that depends," she said. Not exactly the sort of response I was looking for, but she continued. "What do you want to do?"

"If I knew that, I wouldn't be here," I responded, a bit put off by her question. "I used to think maybe I had a future in athletics, but now I'm not so sure. It's not the most stable career, even for the most elite guys. If I'm being honest, I don't know if I have what it takes."

"It takes a lot of maturity to admit that."

"Maybe. I'm not so sure. I just reached a point where my best wasn't good enough any more. Now I don't know what to do."

"There has to be something other than sports that you're passionate about."

"Well," I continued hesitantly, "I've always liked business too, but I'm not sure where to start my career in that."

"That's okay," she said. "These things take time. Why don't you start by taking a look at the things in your life that you enjoy? Then look at the things you have some ability in. Once you find the overlap, you'll have somewhere to start."

After that meeting, I took a survey of my life. I knew I loved sports, but I also knew that I couldn't compete professionally. I had to look somewhere else for an overlap.

Forming a list, I catalogued different things that I was passionate about. The first thing that came to mind was traveling. I loved the trips that I'd take with my family down to Florida and elsewhere. Unfortunately, you can't make a living by going on vacation. I had to dig deeper. What was it about traveling that I liked?

That's when I remembered the sort of luxury that people lived daily in Pompano Beach, and what it felt like to experience just a taste of that lifestyle. That was what appealed to me most about traveling: the way you get treated in a nice hotel, the quality of service at a fine restaurant or at a nice golf course. Suddenly, it all clicked into place. If I could combine that passion for luxury service with the business acumen and people skills I'd fostered during my fireworks and puppy dealing days, then I could make a career of it.

44

A few weeks later, I applied to the Hotel and Resort Administration program at Fanshawe College in London. Grand designs filled my mind. I could picture being the director of an expansive resort or fine hotel. Waking up in the morning and taking in the scope of the property before instructing the staff on their duties.

I would spend the day greeting guests, and the evening checking in with the chef and sampling gourmet creations. Before bed, I would have a chance to peruse the hotel's thriving finances before waking the next morning to do it all again.

Upon entering the program, however, I quickly realized how unrealistic my dream had been. Don't get me wrong, I enjoyed most of my classes and I had a co-op position with a nice hotel.

The problem wasn't with the program, but with my expectations. I imagined that after graduation I would be able to move relatively smoothly into a lower management position. In my naivete, I failed to grasp how long the path before me lay. Assistant night manager, night manager, assistant day manager, manager of a small hotel, assistant night manager at a slightly bigger hotel, the list of positions keeps going on until you reach the top. Along the way, the pay is not amazing, and the hours were very extensive. After a year in the program, I had to ask myself: *is this what I want to want to do with the rest of my life?*

Ultimately, the answer was no.

When I came to that realization, I knew I had to find another career. I'd pursued athletics to no avail and my alternative had only lasted a year. Naturally, it took me a while to figure out what I was going to do next, but I didn't have time for self-pity. Life wasn't going to wait around for me; I had to seize it.

That's how I was raised, especially by Dad. I remember when we were still living back in Waterdown before his business really picked up, he saw that I was upset about something, and I guess he felt like I needed a pep talk. He gathered me and my brother beside him at the dinner table.

"Do you know where you find sympathy in the dictionary?" he asked.

"No," we responded.

"Between shit and syphilis."

I remember looking back on that moment when I was a bit older and laughing. At the time, I just thought to myself, *Dad, I'm only eight years old.* But that was the way Dad saw things. There was no use feeling sorry for yourself. He ingrained that in us at a really young age, which helped me pick myself up after my experience at Fanshawe — even if his teaching method was a bit rough around the edges.

Now that hotel management was officially off the table, I needed to find a new career path fast. Again, I considered my passions and abilities. I was passionate about business; that much I knew for certain by then. I loved buying and selling. The trouble was finding someone who will pay you to buy and sell. And then it hit me.

Sometimes the solution to your problem is so obvious in hindsight that you wonder why it took you so long to think of it in the first place. I wanted to buy and sell on a grand scale. I was good with people. It was right there in front of me.

Not yet twenty-one years old, I started studying real estate.

"I never saw a wild thing sorry
for itself. A small bird will drop frozen dead from
a bough without ever having felt sorry for itself."
— *D.H. Lawrence*

In real estate, I found something I was passionate about which could also earn significant money.

After my first few months, business was going well enough that I was able to buy myself a car, which for me was a sort of a landmark. Like a lot of kids, I got my first car about four years before that at sixteen. My brother and I had both worked summer jobs since we were fourteen, and we had finally had enough money to buy a car to share. We were so excited; I remember flipping through all the *Auto Trader* magazines and cutting out clippings of the cars we wanted to get. Corvettes and Camaros and all sorts of too-fast sports cars you'd expect a sixteen-year-old kid to want.

As we were arranging them all over the dining room table, salivating at the thought of getting behind the wheel of our first car, Dad ambled into the room.

"What are you doing?" he asked.

"Oh, we're organizing ourselves," Greg said. "We're going to buy a car."

"With what?"

"With the money we saved," I said. "Together, we have just enough to get this one!" I proudly pointed at a bright yellow Camaro with black racing stripes.

"Hmm." He left the room without saying another word. The next day, he went out and bought my brother and me a brand-new Ford Tempo with the smallest engine you could possibly get. I guess he figured we were going to kill ourselves if we got one of the cars from the magazines. Greg kept that dinky little car for ages, even after he got married and was making good money. I didn't think it was cool enough, so a year later when I turned seventeen, I bought a black Mazda RX-7.

Dad lent me the money, but I was quick to pay him back. He was a stickler about debt. "Don't live above your means," he used to say all the time. "Don't live above your means!" Well, I kept that advice. I was always quick to pay off any debts I happened to incur and never spend more than I could afford to, but I never stopped dreaming about those gorgeous sports cars dancing before my eyes on our dining room table. That's why, once I was making decent money selling real estate, the first thing I bought was a sharp, new-to-me car.

Of all the vehicles I've owned in my life, that one stands out in my memory: a 1983 Jaguar XJ6, done up exactly the way I wanted it. With after market rims, lightly tinted windows, walnut drop-down tables, navy blue leather seats, and charcoal grey paint that shimmered in the sun. Damn, that was a beautiful car. It wasn't too expensive either. Around that time, Jaguars had dropped a lot in value. They weren't seen as a reliable car, but I didn't care about that. I was young, I had a new job, and I wanted a badass Jag. Of course, Dad didn't see it that way.

"It's no good, getting a car like that," he said. "It looks like you're the president of the company, but you're just starting out. You shouldn't drive that sort of car unless you've earned it."

That was one of my issues with Dad. He said whatever was on his mind, and a lot of the time, his mind seemed to be preoccupied with the possible failings of his children. Me in particular. I was proud of that car and the steps I'd taken to get it. I like to set goals, like getting my real estate license or selling my first house, and I reward myself once I meet those goals. Never in an extravagant way, though. I could afford the car, but Dad didn't really care about that. He just didn't like the sight of his son driving around town in a Jaguar drawing attention to himself. He wanted Greg and me to fit his idea of success, which for him included modesty, and if we didn't, he let us know.

In the back of my mind, it hurt that Dad didn't think I deserved a beautiful car, but I bracketed my irritation. I just had to show him by selling more houses. At the same time, I was trying to keep up a healthy lifestyle. I made sure I never let myself get too out of shape, and I experimented with a lot of different athletic hobbies. Kickboxing, motocross, scuba diving, downhill skiing: each became an obsession of mine for some amount of time.

Sometimes it would be a month, sometimes years. There are quite a few that I still keep up with today. Most significantly, I started dabbling in gymnastics again.

At first, I was mostly just trying to keep in shape. I'd go to Cambridge Olympians, which was a small gym in Cambridge located at the back of the flea market, and jump on the trampoline for a while, nothing too serious. I was only in my early twenties at that point, but I was well past my competing days, and I knew it.

A year passed and I continued training at Cambridge Olympians.

After a while, I even started to help out a group of guys, spotting and offering advice here and there, until I heard from a friend of mine that the Kips had let go of their head trainer.

"And they're bringing in a Russian to replace her," he told me. "Elvira something. Real Soviet training. I can't wait to see what she does with the place."

I didn't really care that much for the previous head coach, so silently I thought, *she can't possibly make it worse,* and for a time I thought that was the end of it. Two more weeks passed before I received a job offer that would change my life.

I had just finished helping some of the boys on the rings and I was ready to head home when a woman approached me from the other side of the gym. "Can I help you?"

"Do you work here?" she asked with an unmistakably Russian accent. Putting two and two together, I realized this must be the new coach of the Kips. Elvira, if I remembered correctly.

"No, not really," I said. "I mean, sometimes I help out, but not for money."

"You know, I've been watching you coach for the past two hours. You look really enthusiastic, you're young, you're strong, and I need someone like that to help me at the gym. Would you be interested in coaching women's gymnastics?"

"Do you mean like a job?" I asked dumbly. I'd never even considered coaching professionally.

"Yes, a job. Part-time, competitive wages. That sort of thing. Are you interested?"

"I've never done anything like that before," I mumbled, half to Elvira and half to myself. "I've only ever worked with the guys, and never for money."

She was undeterred. "It's really quite similar, you know. The acrobatics are the same, the high bar is the same, just add another bar. Please, I really do need a coach to work with the girls. I need a strong man to spot."

"Can you give me some time to think about it?"

"Here's my number," she said, producing a small slip of paper from her front pocket. "Call me if you want the job."

At that point, I already had two jobs. Real estate was still my main focus, but during the nights I was working shifts at an automotive quality control company. Not that I needed the extra hours — I just loved to work! I've always been like that, but even more so in those days. I enjoyed being busy and couldn't stand idleness. Even so, did I really have time for a third job?

I found out later that the whole opportunity had arisen more or less from blind chance. Ever since she started at the Kips, Elvira had been looking to hire a male coach.

"I need a man," she would say to her daughter each day after work. "Someone strong who can spot the girls. Where can I find a man?"

One day her daughter, Liana, decided to go shopping at the flea market with her grandma. They had no idea there was a gym behind all the dingy tents and vendors, let alone a young man who could teach gymnastics.

"Mom, I found you a man!" she said the next time Elvira came home from work.

"Where?"

"At the flea market!" she exclaimed. The two of them burst into laughter, and the rest is history.

I was happy selling real estate. I was making good money, more than I would be as a gymnastics coach, I was sure of that. More than that, I enjoyed being a realtor. I was twenty-two, ambitious — the whole world lay before me. I wasn't about to take a pay cut and tie myself down to some gym. I was sure I'd made the right choice.

Still, something was starting to gnaw on me again in the weeks that followed, that old itch that begged to be scratched. I found that I was racing home after work just so I could grab my bag and head to the gym to coach. The same fire that began when my mom first enrolled me in gymnastics classes in the third grade still burned within me. It had been smoldering in the years since I graduated high school, but the embers never died. The thrill that I'd felt in the heat of a football game, the rush of adrenaline during a hard-fought wrestling match, these were things I couldn't replicate in the world of buying and selling houses.

I realized that this was my chance. I had to seize the moment. Real estate would be waiting in the bleachers in case this crazy plan didn't pan out, but I had to give it a try.

I raced down to the gym and found Elvira standing in the corner observing some promising looking young athletes.

"Hi Elvira, I've had some more time to think. I'd like to take you up on that job offer," I said.

"I appreciate that, but I found someone else." The words thudded in my ears like a dull, hollow echo. "There is no more job opening. Sorry."

"Life is too short for boring cars."

— *Anonymous*

CHAPTER FOUR
The Soviet Invasion

"Because one believes in oneself, one doesn't try to convince others. Because one is content with oneself, one doesn't need others' approval. Because one accepts oneself, the whole world accepts him or her."

— *Lao-Tzu*

Practically everybody at some point reaches a stage in their life when they think they're doing pretty well. Maybe you're there right now. It's not perfect but given all the shit you've had to deal with, life is pretty good. You've got a steady job, a supportive family, and enough money to spoil yourself every now and then.

You figure you've put in the hard work and now it's time to relax and enjoy yourself.

Unfortunately, things don't work that way. I had to learn that lesson the hard way. Even when everything seems to be going your way, after you've spent years building up exactly the sort of life you want, the universe has a nasty habit of dragging you down back to the bedrock. That's one of life's immutable constants, like the monotonous ebb and flow of the ocean tides.

I was crushed, even though I wasn't really sure why. I'd missed out on the coaching job, but so what? I'd been perfectly happy before Elvira ever offered me a job. Why should things be different now? I still had my real estate practice. I still had all my contacts, I still had lots of friends, I still had the life that just last week had seemed to be more than enough for me. So why did everything feel different?

"Hello?"

The voice rattled in my ears, startling me out of my trance.

"Listen, there's got to be something I can do. I didn't realize before, but gymnastics… coaching… this is what I want to do."

"Sorry, but the position has already been filled. I called back one of my old Soviet colleagues and he's going to be here in a couple of months. We're just waiting for the paperwork to go through."

This wasn't the way this was supposed to go. I'd finally discovered my true passion. I couldn't let this opportunity slip through my fingers.

"There's got to be something I can do for you. I can work part-time, evenings, weekends. I just want the experience. To work with someone like you, someone who really knows what they're doing, it would be an honour."

"Oh?" The faintest hint of a smirk tugged at the corners of her lips. "I didn't get that impression when we met. I watched you work for hours, and you didn't even notice me."

"Ya I, um, read an article about you in the newspaper," I said sheepishly. "And I kind of realized what I would be missing out on."

Earlier that week, the *Cambridge Times* had run a front-page article about Elvira. Turns out she was Elvira Saadi, a double Olympic Gold Medalist and world-class gymnastics coach. And I didn't know her from Adam. The second I first saw that article I thought, *Oh, shit, I just blew that.*

"I suppose there might be some work you could do for us," she said. "But it wouldn't be full-time—"

"That's fine."

"—and you wouldn't be working with the top athletes."

"Of course."

"And you'd have to be serious. No slacking off."

"Never!"

After a pause I thought would never end, she uttered a single word that let the air back into the room: "Okay."

I'd nearly let my dream job pass me by, but just as it looked like I'd made the sort of mistake that haunts you for the rest of your life, I managed to snatch victory from the jaws of defeat.

For the next few months, I worked part-time at the Cambridge Kips. Right off the bat, they threw me into the deep end. I worked every day with a group of kids

— mostly at the lower level — that she didn't have time to coach, but their skill level didn't matter to me; I was just excited to be coaching, period. Every time I entered the gym, I knew I was going to learn something new. Some of that experience came from working with the kids themselves, but a lot of it also came from just observing the coaches and the way they worked.

Later, when the male coach she'd hired arrived, I had even more information to draw from. His name was Vladimir Kondratenko, and he'd known Elvira from their days back in the Soviet Union.

Between the two of them, I had a wealth of knowledge exceeding anything an aspiring coach could ask for, and I made sure to take advantage of the opportunity.

"Can you show me this…"

"Can you teach me that…"

I was a constant nuisance, bugging them all the time about how to improve my coaching. At first, Elvira was a bit apprehensive about teaching me some of the 'Soviet secrets'.

"Don't show him the advanced techniques, he's not ready!" she would say to Vladimir, but I was persistent. If she was worried about my commitment, she'd soon learn just how serious I was about coaching. Day after day, I strove not just to do enough, but to excel. To that end, I even started coming in on my days off just to watch them work and ask questions. Whether I was being paid or not didn't matter, the experience was more important to me. I wanted to be the best and to do that, I had to put in the time and the effort beyond what others would consider sufficient.

It was that ambitious attitude that eventually won them over. We were driven to improve.

With Vladimir, it was natural, and our relationship was easy. Dispel any notions you might have about cold, emotionless Russian coaches and athletes. Vladimir was as kind a man as I'd ever known. Within a few days of arriving in Canada, Vladimir Kondratenko the masterful Soviet gymnastics trainer had vanished, replaced simply by good-natured Vladi. Even more so than Elvira, Vladi was selfless when it came to sharing his knowledge. Whatever questions I had; he was eager to answer them.

After nearly a year working part-time with the two of them, I knew it was time to take the next step. I figured if I was serious about coaching, and I was increasingly sure that I was, then I needed to commit all of my time. I had been working as a realtor the whole time I was with the Kips, but the more experience I got coaching, the harder it got to justify the split. I loved coaching. I was good at coaching. So why was I spending most of my time selling houses?

In 1997, six years after I dropped out of college to get my real estate license, I quit my day job and enrolled at Seneca College for a diploma in Advanced Coaching Techniques for Women's Gymnastics. In that year, I studied under some fantastic professors and industry experts while still coaching back at the Kips on weekends. I was completely immersed in all aspects of coaching for eight hours a day, seven days a week. I was doing training sessions in the morning then spending all day in class and most evenings doing high-performance training. Sunrise to sunset, gymnastics took over my life. And I loved it.

After I graduated, I returned to work with Elvira and Vladi full time at Kips. I was free to pour all my focus into gymnastics, just like it had been when I was a kid. It was different this time, of course. Helping others achieve their goals requires a different sort of attitude compared to doing things for yourself. There are more nuances, different ways to approach teaching in different circumstances and with different personality types. No two situations are ever the same and no single approach works best.

Still, despite the differences, my full-fledged return to gymnastics felt like a homecoming. It stirred something inside me that had long lay dormant. The same drive for perfection, the same physical effort, the same singular determination. Real estate had been good to me, and I have fond memories from that time in my life, but I had always been missing the thrill of competition and the rush of satisfaction that comes from realizing athletic potential. I had finally found what I was meant to do!

My father, unfortunately, didn't see it that way.

"Why the Hell would you leave a steady job in real estate to teach kids to cartwheel?"

Teaching gymnastics just wasn't something grown men did in his eyes. His sons should have responsible, respectable jobs, ideally something in business, like him. No matter how much success I achieved in my coaching, I always felt like I was coming up short.

Maybe in his eyes, I should have been more like my brother. Now, I love my brother, but he can be a pain-in-the-ass act to follow. Even when we were growing up, he seemed to never put a foot wrong. He was uber-responsible, super smart, great in school, a good athlete — pretty much a parents' dream. Plus, he was damn cool to boot. I mean, he got his pilot's license when he was fifteen years old. Who does that? To top it all off, when it came time to choose a career, he ended up following in Dad's footsteps. These days, he's the president of a massive industrial construction company in Burlington. So, pretty much he's everything a parent could dream of.

Whenever he would introduce us, Dad would say, "This is my Number Two Son, Aaron." In hindsight, I know he didn't mean it in a demeaning way, but that's always how I took it. It was like a permanent sign hanging around my neck: Number Two Son. No matter what I did, it felt like I was coming in second. Buy a nice car? Number Two Son. Twenty-three years old and still renting an apartment? Number Two Son. Quit a career in real estate and started coaching women's gymnastics? Definitely a number-two-son move.

I knew I was going to be a damned good coach, but at that point, I don't know how much that mattered to Dad. I started to push myself harder than ever before. I was going to become so successful in coaching that even Dad would acknowledge it.

For the next seven years, I worked at Kips under Elvira and Vladi honing my craft. I earned additional coaching certifications. I developed a strong reputation in the gymnastics community. I did everything I could think of to show my dad and anyone who had ever doubted me, that I belonged among the best of the best.

I still remember when I called him to say that I was going to quit my job to pursue gymnastics coaching full-time.

"I don't understand why you won't at least keep the real estate license," he said at the end of a lengthy phone call.

We'd had the same conversation dozens of times before. He was always telling me I needed to be more serious, to work harder. To be more like him, I thought, though he would never say that. My decision to pursue a career in gymnastics was just the latest example in a long series of life choices that seemed to puzzle him. Now I'd finally had enough.

"Listen, Dad. Do you think Bela Karolyi sells real estate on the side?"

There was a long, dead silence. Then I hung up. I was tired of trying to measure up to his expectations, or to anybody else's for that matter. At that moment, I stopped giving a damn what everybody else thought about my career. I was going to be a gymnastics coach, the best one in Canada, and Dad was just going to have to deal with it.

I pushed on, determined to go even further in gymnastics coaching. I'd been working at the Kips for seven years now, during which time I'd established a reputation as one of the rising elite coaches in Canadian gymnastics. I was also receiving head-coach job offers almost every month from different clubs, but up until then, I'd been reluctant to leave the Kips, Elvira, and Vladi.

Eventually, though, it was time to move on. If I wanted to be the best coach in Canada, I had to branch off on my own, so I left Kips with Elvira's blessing and took a head coaching job in Toronto. It was a great opportunity, and I enjoyed the time I spent in that position, but I soon realized I was ready for even greater responsibilities. I was ready to open my own gym.

Serendipitously, around the same time, I met the love of my life, Angela. After six months of dating, we were engaged, and from there all the pieces of a beautiful picture started falling into place. Angela was a gymnastics coach too — a fantastic one at that — my perfect partner in life and in business. In March 2004 we got married, and by June of that year, we'd opened Revolution Gymnastics and Sports Centre in Waterloo.

Almost immediately, business at Revolution picked up and soon we were coaching athletes all the way from beginners to advanced competitors. By 2007, we had gymnasts competing at the elite level, and Angela and I were expecting our first child, a beautiful girl named Ava. I had a thriving business and an amazing family.

Everything was going so well. Everything, that is, except for a close and real relationship with my dad.

Let me just say first that I love my dad. There are tons of things I admire about him, and I've looked up to him my entire life. He's tough, funny, fearless, and hard-working.

For a very long time, I've been trying to get his attention, to make him see that there are more important things in life than work and his idea of success. In every county wrestling match, in every seventy-hour work week, in every coaching gig or business venture in the back of my mind, I was hoping that this time he'd see.

His obsession with work and success was an addiction. It was a disease, and soon enough, like all diseases, it spread.

As far back as I can remember, Dad drank a lot. Too much. It got worse the older I got, and by the time I was seventeen years old, he was a full-blown alcoholic. Those were the worst years when I was in my late teens, early twenties. He smelled of liquor at all hours and pretty much any time he wasn't at work was spent drinking himself into a stupor.

Alcohol became yet another suitor for his affections, and again, I found I couldn't compete. In those formative years, right as I had to decide what I was going to do with my life and what kind of man I wanted to become, Dad practically disappeared from my life. At that time, I felt like I would never be as important to him as his work or his drink.

If I had it rough, Mom had it ten times worse. It took the patience of a saint to put up with his drinking for as long as she did, but eventually, even she'd had enough, and they divorced in 1989.

Even the breakdown of his marriage didn't force him to get his act together though. If anything, he got worse.

A few years after the split, he drank himself silly in his house and fell into an alcoholic seizure. He slumped over, unable to move his arms to brace his fall, and slammed his head on the edge of the fireplace brickwork. The swelling in his brain was so severe he had to have surgery, but he survived.

He has a very long scar down the back of his head now where they had to slice open his skull to relieve the swelling, a constant reminder of how close his disease came to ending his life. I suppose scars are something else we have in common, though mine came much later and under very different circumstances.

After his brush with death, Dad finally sobered up for good.

That was over twenty-five years ago now. For a while, he had some speech problems, but today I'd say he's recovered about 99%. He's remarried now and is still working sixty hours a week. I'm happy for him. He turned his life around after the accident, and that's no small feat.

In 2009, Angela and I decided to move Revolution to a new, bigger, state-of-the-art facility. After years of hard work, we'd finally made it big. The paper ran a huge article about us, on the front page of the business section, which prompted Dad to give me a call.

"I was just reading the business section of the *K-W Record*, and I saw you right there on the front page. Congratulations. I'm really proud of you."

We chatted for a bit longer, then I hung up. As I sat down later that night to go over the company finances, Dad's words kept running through my mind, and the more I thought about it, the more it upset me. *It takes me getting on the front page of the business section of the newspaper for you to call me and tell me I'm doing okay? Really? That article came out five years after Angela and I opened Revolution.*

It didn't matter that I told him in a hundred different ways that I was doing well in the career I chose. But if the business section of the *K-W Record* says so, well then, I must be doing all right.

I was determined to improve myself too, but that proved more difficult in practice.

I want to live my life for myself, I thought. Not for Dad or for anybody else except me and my family. No more pressure to live up to other people's expectations. I'm just going to live my life.

If only it were that easy. The patterns ingrained in me since those carefree days in Waterdown proved impossible to break. No matter how hard I tried not to, I still saw life as a grand competition, and I was going to win.

Consciously or unconsciously, the pressure of expectations weighed heavily on my shoulders at every competition. I wasn't ready then to change my way of thinking. Ultimately, it would take a cataclysmic event, a heart-racing 240 beats per minute, and a whole lot of time feeling like absolute shit to turn my life around. My hope is that by listening to my story, you can at least avoid that last part.

I'm reminded of something Elvira used to say when I first started working at the Kips. "There are some things that you'll never figure out on your own, and I'll tell you those secrets. There are other things that you have to figure out on your own, and I'll never tell you those things." Hopefully, this book can help you with the things you might not have been able to figure out on your own.

Ultimately, though, it's up to you to uncover the truths about yourself.

Just keep in mind: the more we value things outside our control, the less control we have.

— Epictetus

CHAPTER FIVE
Be Still My Beating Heart

I'm not going to die here.

It was almost too absurd. I couldn't die there, buckled onto a gurney in the back of an ambulance hurtling its way to the nearest hospital in Trois-Rivières. Not after everything was finally going so well. Not now that I had a beautiful family waiting for me back home and a thriving business that depended on me. Not now that I'd discovered my passion and forged a successful career from it. Not after all the shit I had been through trying to prove myself.

There was no way in hell I was going to let all that go.

Angela, Gavin, Ava: I couldn't leave them. I couldn't die. I had too much to live for.

By the time we reached the hospital, I'd calmed myself down mentally, but my heart was still racing: 240 beats per minute the ambulance monitors said. Then, just as we pulled into the ER entrance, as suddenly as it had begun, the attack subsided.

Holy shit I'm really not going to die here.

I had no clue what just happened to me or why it stopped. I only knew one thing for sure: I was fucking tired. The thousands of questions swirling in my mind would have to wait. EMS attendants wheeled my gurney to an examination room where I was transferred onto one of the hospital beds. It was cold, hard, and the most welcome bed I'd ever felt.

I lay as still as a statue until the doctor entered the room.

"Hello," he said. "My name is Dr Gauthier. How are you feeling?"

"I'm okay," I said.

"Hmm, yes," he said, glancing down at a file folder he held in his hand. "Have you experienced anything like this before?"

At the time, I never thought to draw the connection between the strange feeling in my neck when I wrestled or my racing pulse during gym class and what I'd just experienced. This was orders of magnitude more intense. It was like nothing I'd ever felt before, except…

"Yes, once. One time just a couple of weeks ago," I said, the memory rushing back to me as I spoke. "I was at a gymnastics meet, in Pennsylvania." Dr Gauthier raised an eyebrow.

"I went over to the corner. I had to lean against the wall to support myself. I didn't know what was happening, but I had this feeling in my neck like something beating really quickly, so I checked my heart rate monitor and it said 230, 235. I did the same thing today and it was around 240."

"EMS measured your heart rate at 245."

"Ya, so at the time I thought that was really high. It lasted for about ten or fifteen minutes and then it stopped. The first thing I did when I got home was Google what the maximum heart rate should be for a guy my age. I can't remember what exactly it was, but I was way, way above it."

"A rate of 120 to 150 would be fairly normal for someone doing exercise."

"Exactly. I thought there must be something wrong, so I went to my family doctor once I got back to Canada. I had this Elite Canada gymnastics meet here in Trois-Rivières, and I was worried something might happen again. But he said I was okay to go. I guess I was right to be worried," I said. "What's going on with me?"

"I believe you have a heart condition known as supraventricular tachycardia or SVT." He jotted a few notes on a piece of paper before continuing.

"I'm going to give you some pills to take. They're called metoprolol. Take two a day, one in the morning and one in the evening, and that should prevent major attacks. We're going to hold you for the night and monitor your condition. Right now, you seem to be in stable condition. Assuming you don't have another episode, I'm going to release you tomorrow morning. Give this to your doctor back home," he added, offering me the piece of paper in his hand. "It covers all the information they should need to assess your case moving forward, including the measurements EMS personnel took while you were in the ambulance. There are treatment options available, but that's something you should be discussing with your doctor first and then, ideally, with a specialist. For now, just get some rest."

"Thank you, Doctor," I replied. "I will."

I caught a flight back to Toronto the very next day. My brother Greg picked me up from the airport and drove me the rest of the way home. He was a calming presence. I imagine he was probably worried about me, but he did a good job hiding it.

Angela, on the other hand, let me know right away how she felt about the whole ordeal.

I arrived home around two in the afternoon and the first thing I saw was her smile. "I'm so glad you're home," she said. "I'm so happy you're okay. I love you."

I'd called her as soon as I could to let her know what had happened. During the call, I'd tried to downplay the severity of the incident as much as I could, but she knew it was bad. Your husband doesn't usually call you in the middle of the night from a hospital in Trois-Rivières with good news.

"It's all right," I said. "I'm fine now. I scheduled an appointment with Dr Harris for tomorrow. We'll go together to meet with him, and you'll see that this is nothing to get worked up about."

"I'm just glad you're home," she repeated. I don't know whether she saw through my confident facade or not, but at that moment, I didn't care. Holding Angela in my arms, I forgot about Trois- Rivières and SVT. I was together with my beautiful wife, stroking her long, dark hair as I clutched her tightly. I could feel her breath on my shoulder, deep and soft, like a warm breeze calling a sailor home after a long voyage.

I was home and that was all that mattered.

The next day, we went to see Dr Harris. He'd been my GP ever since Angela and I first moved to Waterloo, but up until now, I'd never had any serious medical conditions for him to treat. He was also the doctor who said I was fine to go to Trois-Rivières, so you can imagine how confident I was in his professional opinion. Still, he was my doctor, and I wanted to talk to someone as soon as possible to discuss treatments.

As we waited for Dr Harris in the examination room, I had some time to study the room around me. In many ways, it was remarkably similar to the room in Trois-Rivières. The same antiseptic blue paint on the walls, the same too-clean smell, the same uncomfortable bed.

And yet, it somehow felt different, and not because of any physical peculiarity. No, the difference was in me. Then, I had been caked in sweat and exhausted from my ordeal. I was terrified but also thrilled to be alive. Now, everything spoke to me of death. This was a place sick people came. Why should I lie down on the rock-hard bed? I wasn't sick. I felt fine.

But I was sick. I was horribly sick. Only two days ago, I had thought I might die crumpled in a heap on a gymnasium floor. Something was seriously wrong with me, and I still didn't understand how it had happened, or why, or even what it was. *SVT*. It was like a shadow that haunted me now, an intrinsic part of who I was but always shrouded in darkness.

What had happened to the confident little boy who jumped from the roof of his childhood home just to see if he could fly? He was gone, along with the indestructible wrestling champion and invincible gymnastics talent. For the first time in my life, I felt truly old. My body, which had served me so well for the past forty years, was betraying me.

Why now? Was it from the stress of trying to live up to my dad's expectations? Was it because I hadn't been taking very good care of myself these past few years? I had no idea, and it didn't seem like my doctor did either. He'd sent me to a gymnastics meet even after I told him about what happened in Pennsylvania.

All I knew was that I was terrified, and I wanted answers. At last, the doctor arrived.

"So, what seems to be the problem today?" he asked.

"It's my heart," I said. "As I told you last time, it just races uncontrollably. It happened again when I was in Quebec, only worse this time."

"I see," he said. "What happened exactly?"

"I was coaching when—" I froze. A familiar pulse coursed through my neck. *Not again*!

"It was… I can feel it right now. My heart goes into overdrive. Beats so fast I can't even count it. It's just… I can feel it, pounding like you wouldn't believe. So fast. It's too fast, I can't…" I trailed off, trying to find the words that would make him understand.

"Are you all right?!" he asked.

I was panting now, trying to catch my breath.

Angela interjected. "He's having another attack!"

The doctor rushed to my side and put fingers to my neck. His fingers were trembling nearly as bad as my own.

"I, um, I don't — okay, I'm going to call the ambulance," he said. "Nurse!" he shouted. "Call 9-11, it's an emergency." I could scarcely imagine words that would inspire less confidence in a patient.

"It's going to be okay, honey," Angela said, stroking my hand. I wanted to believe her, but the trembling in her voice gave her away.

"He's in SVT," I heard one of the EMTs say to his partner. "Quick, help me load him onto the gurney."

"SVT?" Doctor Harris muttered, flushed in the face, as he left the room.

"You're going to be okay." Angela tried to comfort me. For a moment, I almost believed her, but then the pounding in my chest convinced me otherwise.

It had only been a few minutes, but I knew what was going to happen. I'd been down this road before, and it got a lot worse before it got better. My heart was an engine about to explode and there was nothing I could do about it.

Boom-boom-boom, the pistons fired. *Boom-boom-boom.* Faster and faster, like the heavy echo of machine-gun fire.

Boom-boom-boom-boom-boom-boom. Onto the gurney.

Boom-boom-boom-boom-boom-boom-boom. Into the ambulance. *Boom-boom-boom-boom-boom-boom-boom-boom-boom.* And towards a bright light?

Boom-boom-boom-boom-boom-boom-boom-boom-boom-boom-boom-boom-boom-boom-boom-boom-boom-boom-boom-boom.

"Aaron," a voice said, dragging me back to reality. I glanced over to the paramedic who had spoken. "We're going to have to give you a dose of adenosine. When it hits you, everything's going to come to a stop. Do you understand? Your heart is going to feel like it stops. Then it's going to start again. It's not going to feel good, but this is what has to happen."

"Yes, okay," I said. Anything to stop the racing beats.

"If the first dose doesn't work, we're going to double the dose," he said.

"And if that's not enough?" I asked.

"Then we might have to use the defibrillator to reboot your heart."

Now I was fucking terrified. I had no clue what adenosine was, but I knew for damn sure I didn't want to get shocked with the paddles. That was always the last resort on the doctor shows that Angela watched, and it didn't usually end well.

First, though, they tried the regular dose of adenosine. And boy, they weren't kidding. Almost as soon as the needle broke my skin, my whole body went numb, and blackness encroached at the corners of my vision. I felt like my entire body was being sucked into an enormous pillow, like a wisp of cloud melting away into an endless blue sky.

Then it was over. That's how the drug works. In a matter of seconds, it gets absorbed by your body and the effect dissipates, hopefully restoring your heart to working order in the process.

Only it didn't. Just a handful of seconds after the adenosine wore off, I could feel it again, *boom-boom-boom-boom*, the sound of my heart pounding 240 times every minute. "It didn't take!" the EMS shouted, "double the dosage!"

They doubled the dose and tried again. This was it. Either it works, or I get shocked. *Please, please let it work*, I thought. Then it hit me like a tonne of bricks. I melted, and this time when I came back to my body, my heart was beating in a normal rhythm. I couldn't believe it: it actually worked.

We arrived at St Mary's hospital in Kitchener and the EMTs rolled my gurney out of the ambulance. The wheels had scarcely hit the ground when Angela rushed to meet me, though I wasn't exactly sure where she came from. Had she been with me the whole time in the ambulance, or had she been following in a separate car? I wasn't sure. It was as if a thick fog had clouded my brain, but it didn't matter any more. We were together again, and I had survived. For the time being, anyway.

Boom-boom. Less than two hours after the last attack subsided, I felt it again. *Boom-boom-boom.* The turbo engine that I thought was dead had merely stalled. Lying in the waiting room to see yet another doctor, I was hit with another attack.

"Adenosine, six units!" I heard someone shout, though I couldn't be sure who. I felt the needle prick my skin and the now-familiar melting sensation. Then, nothing. My heartbeat maintained its furious pace.

This was my third dose over the past few hours. I didn't know much about SVT, or the drugs used to treat it, but even I knew I was nearing my breaking point. There was only so much more my body could take. They were preparing one more boosted dosage of adenosine, and if that didn't work, then no amount of drugs was going to work. Then I heard a doctor utter the words that still ring in my nightmares:

"Mrs Brokenshire, you need to leave the room. Now."

For a split second, she froze, her wide eyes staring blankly through the doctor's face. Then, without a word, she turned, cast a loving glance in my direction, and exited the room.

There is only one reason for a doctor to ask a wife to leave the room, and we all knew what that was. This wasn't like Pennsylvania or even Trois-Rivières. This was the end of the line. Suddenly, I saw the picture in crystal clarity. *Right here, in this room, I'm either going to die, or I'm going to live.* They gave me the final dose and I closed my eyes.

I could feel the heat of the bright lights hanging over my bed, but I kept my eyes closed.

And I thought to myself, *please, let me live. God, if you're up there, I want to live.*

At that moment, my thoughts were on one thing. I didn't worry about anything past or future. I had one thought: a pure, timeless, unconscious, indivisible, unstoppable thought: I want to live. In that crystallized sliver of time, nothing else existed. Not SVT, not fear, not depression, not anxiety, not disappointment. Not any of the things that might bother you or me.

I want to live. That's all that there is to it. That's the beginning, and if you take that as your starting point, there's no telling where you might end up.

CHAPTER SIX
A Diagnosis of Decisions

"How do you feel?"

It had been nearly an hour since the last dose of adenosine.

Thankfully, no paddles were needed.

"Good. Fantastic, all things considered, but I don't think I can take any more of these attacks. There's got to be something I can do about this SVT thing."

I met the doctor's eyes and it occurred to me that I didn't know his name. The past few days were a blur of hospitals, ambulances and men in white coats. He'd probably told me his name when he entered the room, but I didn't remember.

Dr Greene, I read from his name badge.

"There are a few treatment options," he said, "but first I need to know what caused your most recent attack."

I explained to him what had happened, how I'd been fine that morning, but when I got to my GP's office, I started to relive what had happened at Trois-Rivières. Throughout my story, he nodded along approvingly until I came to the second attack. Then his brows scrunched together, and I could tell he had something on his mind.

"Stress can certainly aggravate SVT," he said, "but I'm surprised that you had two such powerful attacks in rapid succession. Didn't your doctor prescribe metoprolol after the first attack?"

"Um, ya, he gave me some pills. I think he said they were metoprolol."

"And did you take them?"

My eyes fell to the floor as I fidgeted with my suddenly restless hands, spinning my wedding band around and around my finger.

"Well... yes," I said. "After the attack, I took a pill. And the next day. I seldom take pills. Not even aspirin, Tylenol, those sorts of things. I don't like putting things into my body that aren't, you know, natural."

"So, you didn't take any metoprolol today?"

"They didn't really explain to me what the pills did. They just said, 'take these pills', but the pills — the metoprolol or whatever — weren't making me feel very good. I was really drowsy, and my head didn't feel right, so I figured I would hold off on taking any more until I spoke to my GP. It was only one day."

"Well, I'm telling you now: you've got to keep taking the pills. Your SVT is caused by an excess of electrical nodes and activity around your heart. Metoprolol helps reduce that excess activity and reduces your chances of having such dramatic and severe SVT events."

"So what? I've got to keep taking these pills for the rest of my life!"

"I've scheduled you an appointment with Dr Park. He's an arrhythmia specialist at St. Mary's hospital, one of the best. You'll be in excellent hands."

Great, another doctor.

At that point, I was starting to get fed up with my whole predicament. Illness, I could handle. Give me something to fight and I'll fight it tooth and nail. Uncertainty though, that was the real killer.

For the past few days, I had barely slept. I'd been up all night asking myself questions: *What was wrong with my body? Why was this happening all of the sudden? What could I do about it?* Each question was met with resounding silence.

I knew I had SVT. Dr Gauthier at Trois-Rivières had told me as much. But what the hell did that mean? I avoided doing much research on my own — I found out long ago that you can drive yourself mad looking up symptoms online. Dr Wikipedia will have you convinced you've got brain cancer when 99% of the time it's just a headache. So I waited until I had a chance to talk to a specialist about SVT… my GP had no idea what SVT even was, and now this other doctor — *Dr Greene*, I reminded myself — was referring me to yet another doctor.

"Please, there has to be something you can do. I'll drive myself crazy waiting for another appointment."

"I'm sorry. SVT is a complicated condition. It can manifest in several different forms with various treatment options. You would be better off talking with Dr Park about your unique situation."

"I understand. It's just—" Words failed me. I wanted to say that I'd always led a healthy lifestyle, and athletics were still a huge part of my life — that I couldn't just give that up. But I couldn't coach gymnastics if my heart rate exploded every time I got stressed.

I wanted to tell him that I'd finally found my passion, the thing I'd spent my whole professional life searching for. I wanted to say that I wasn't ready to give that up, that I couldn't let the girls down, couldn't lose my livelihood. That I couldn't have a heart condition.

I wanted to say that I'd never had serious health issues before, that my brother had the same genes as I did, and he was perfectly healthy. I wanted to say that I still had so much more to do, that I still had to live up to my potential.

I wanted to explain all those things, but I couldn't. All I could say, in a weak, tired voice, was:

"Why is this happening to me?"

I'd meant the question to be rhetorical, but after a moment of dead silence, Dr Greene responded.

"Nobody knows exactly what causes SVT," he said. "Approximately 1 in 500 people get SVT, and 1 in 18 people have arrhythmia at some point in their life. Some of them are healthy, some aren't. Some are old, some are young. Some are rich, some are poor. There's nothing you could have done to prevent it."

Nothing I could have done. I suppose he meant that to be some sort of consolation, and maybe it would have been if I was ready to hear it, but at that point, I was just pissed off and confused.

Nothing I could do? Fuck that. I'd been taking charge of my life ever since I was a kid. Sometimes there were challenges — there always are if you're passionate about what you do — but I always pushed through them. Not nailing a gymnastics routine? Practice till my whole body ached. Lacking experience coaching? Go back to school and work my butt off. Feeling a bit complacent? Build a gym from the ground up, just me, my wife, and a whole lot of sweat, blood, and tears. There was nothing I couldn't do if I set my mind to it. At least, that's what I'd always thought.

There's nothing you could have done.

My appointment with the specialist, Dr Park, wasn't scheduled for another three weeks, during which time those words hung over me like a dark cloud. No matter how much I tried to clear my mind, I couldn't stop thinking about SVT. I replayed all the decisions I'd ever made; imagined all the complications that might arise in the future. I was obsessed, and the first casualty of my obsession was sleep.

Taking metoprolol every day certainly didn't help matters. The pills never agreed with me, simultaneously sapping me of energy and keeping me awake long into the night. At first, I didn't notice any major changes in my life, but as the days and weeks dragged on, the sleepless nights started taking a toll on me. When I woke in the morning after a fitful sleep, it felt like I'd been running all night. I didn't have the energy to go to work — I barely had the energy to get out of bed!

And that was on the nights that I could get any sleep in the first place. As often as not, I was up all night tossing and turning, playing and replaying a thousand different scenarios in my over-anxious mind. Between the meds and my constant overthinking, I was lucky if I got a couple hours each night.

By the time I finally got to see Dr Park, I was a wreck physically and emotionally. The night before had been one of the sleepless ones and I was feeling the effects as I sat in the waiting room at St. Mary's. My only consolation was that I could see the end in sight now. I was going to talk with the doctor and finally, we could start doing something about this condition. No more waiting. No more wondering. Now there was something I could actually do.

"What are my options, Doctor?" I asked practically the moment he walked through the door.

For the past three weeks, I'd been building up an image of this man in my mind. Now that I actually saw him, he was taller than I'd expected, and we had a great talk about SVT and me.

"Well, I've been reviewing your file, and there are two main options I can recommend," he said.

"First, I could prescribe you an increased dosage of metoprolol. If you continue taking the prescribed amount every day, then you shouldn't experience any major SVT events. With this option, you should be able to perform most of your daily activities with little to no disruption. However, we will have to increase the prescription every few years as your body becomes accustomed to the metoprolol, and also, you wouldn't be able to perform especially strenuous physical activities."

"And the other option?" I asked, eager to hear what the alternative was.

"The second option is heart surgery."

I swallowed hard.

My heart skipped a beat — which, in my present condition, probably wasn't the best thing. *Heart surgery*? I was only 42 years old. Forty-two-year-olds don't get heart surgery. Heart surgery was the last resort, something people did when they ran out of other options. No, there *had* to be something else I could do. I opened my mouth to speak, but all the words I wanted to say caught in my throat. Unable to utter a sound, I just stared at the man who, only a few seconds ago, I thought was going to make all my problems go away.

"Now I know heart surgery can sound intimidating—"

No shit, I thought.

"—but there has been tremendous progress made in recent decades when it comes to surgical treatments of

SVT. Twenty years ago, this was open-heart surgery. Today, though, we can perform the surgery by way of ablation."

Seeing my eyes glaze over, Dr Park gestured towards a diagram of the human body. "Essentially, what we do is make two incisions, one in your upper leg and one by your collarbone that we would use for a camera and the ablator itself. With the ablator, we burn the extra node that is creating the excess electrical impulses near the main node in your heart."

Heart surgery, burning nodes, ablators and cameras running all throughout my body...

"Are those the only two options?"

"Unfortunately, yes."

"The surgery — what sort of risks are involved in that?"

"It's a fairly common procedure. If you decide to pursue that form of treatment, I will direct you to University Hospital in London. They have a world-class facility there dedicated to heart conditions including SVT. They perform many of these same surgeries every day.

"Now, that being said, there are always risks associated with surgery that you need to be aware of. These can range from infection, pain, and bleeding up to more serious complications such as blood clots or a heart attack."

"But could I die from something like this?"

"Cardiac ablation is not a high-risk surgery, but it's still heart surgery. The possibility of such a negative outcome is minuscule, but not nonexistent."

"Of course, of course," I said half-heartedly. A fog had descended over my mind, enshrouding my conscious thought with streaks of jet black. Death lurked in the corners of my sleep-deprived brain, covering the whole room with a foreboding atmosphere so dense I wondered how I could still breathe. I suppose the metoprolol was good for something after all because I didn't have an SVT event. I was just lost in the dreamlike labyrinth of my own thoughts.

Dimly I noticed that Dr Park was still speaking to me.

"…time to talk over the options with your wife."

"Yes, she had to work today, but I'll talk with her tonight. We run a gym and somebody's got to manage the day-to-day with me — you know. I really don't know what I'd do without her."

"Certainly. Contact the hospital when you've made your decision and we'll move forward from there."

"Thank you, Doctor," I said.

The drive home was one of the longest of my life, but by the time I got home I had all but made up my mind. I was scared as hell. I didn't want to get heart surgery. I didn't want to put Angela and the kids through that. But more than anything else, I knew that I couldn't keep going the way I was going.

I had a gymnastics business to run with thirty-plus employees depending on me. I had young kids at home who needed their dad back, not some shadow of his former self. I needed to be able to run, lift, jump, and I wasn't going to be able to do that if I was up to my eyeballs in metoprolol. The people who took that option made it work for them, but I couldn't live that way. There were risks involved in the surgery, but if I didn't get it done, I knew for sure that my life as I knew it was over.

When I got home, I talked over the options with Angela, and by the end of the night, my decision was final. She wasn't too impressed that I made my decision so quickly, but in the end, we both knew it was the right thing to do.

I thought at the time that I'd just finished the tough part. My enemy was no longer a mystery; I had SVT and I knew exactly what I was going to do about it. I would get the surgery, and everything would be back to normal.

What I didn't realize was that this was just the beginning. There was no way I could imagine the difficulties I'd face over the next few months. As my life spiraled out of control and I descended further and further into the darkest time in my life, I wished above all that I had some sort of guide, something to help me understand what was happening to me. Some sort of advice from someone who'd been to that dark place and survived.

Well, now I'm here to tell you: I was there. I felt my whole world crumble around me, exposing all of my faults and mistakes, my arrogance and my short-sightedness. And I survived. More than that, I found answers to questions I didn't even know I was asking. If you want to learn how, read on.

He who fears death will never do anything worth of a man who is alive.

— Lucius Annaeus Seneca

A great picture of my dad back in the day

Me, My dad and Greg at a company picnic in 1972

Left to right: My brother Greg, me (seated), Dad, our fishing guide - Welesley, Grandma Serafin, Mom. Jamaica 1976

The kindest, gentlest person I've
known. Vladimr Kondratenko. An
amazing coach, mentor and friend.
Rest in peace, Vladi.

Our first Provincial Championships
in Thunder Bay with my teammate
Mark Hudson, 1981

Lawson and me on the competition
floor, 2012

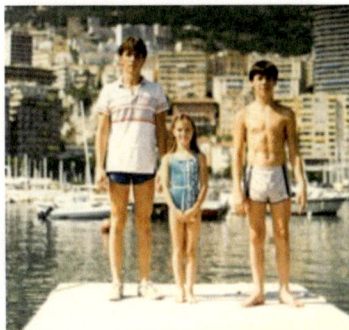

Greg, Leah and me on a family
vacation in Europe, 1984

The Atlanta Olympic Games just as the competition concluded with Elvira and Yvonne Tousek, 1996

Flipping around at the beach, 2015

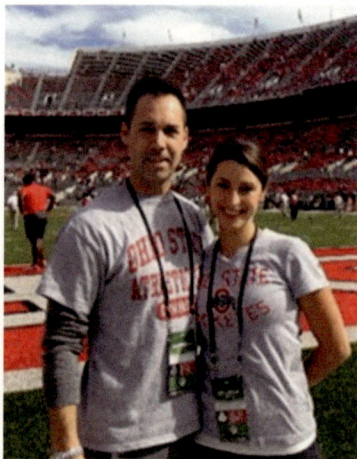

Angela and me at an Ohio State football game. We were invited after having two of our gymnasts receive full athletic scholarships there.

Doing a pre scuba dive check in the pool with baby Ava, 2009

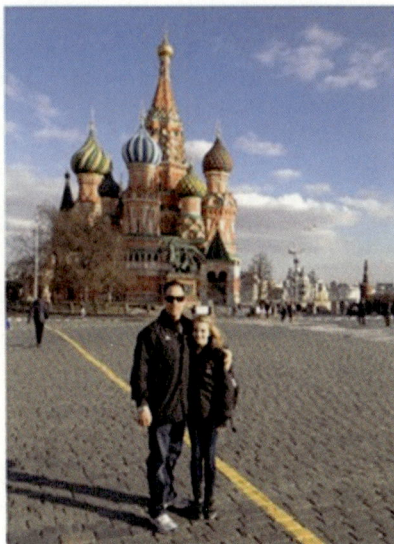

Standing in Red Square after a national team training camp in Moscow

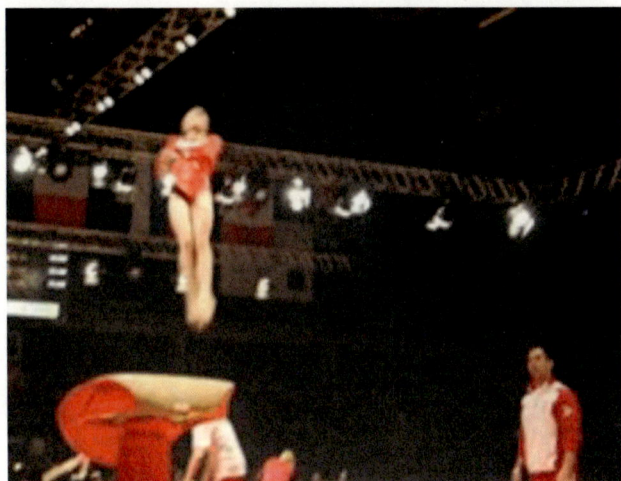

Coaching vault at an international contest in Marseille, France, 2011

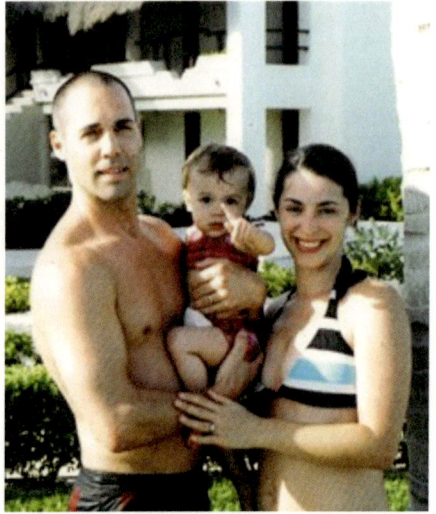

Me, Angela and Ava in Mexico, 2008

Angela and I in Mexico enjoying the sun and surf

With Ava at the cottage

Coaching at the Youth Olympics in Nanjing, China, with Sydney Townsend

Our young family

Ava and Gavin

*Coming out of the water.
"Rockin' my Tri" in Macon,
Georgia, 2016*

Winning the KPnP Taekwondo Open in 2017, It was the first combative tournament I entered after my heart surgery.

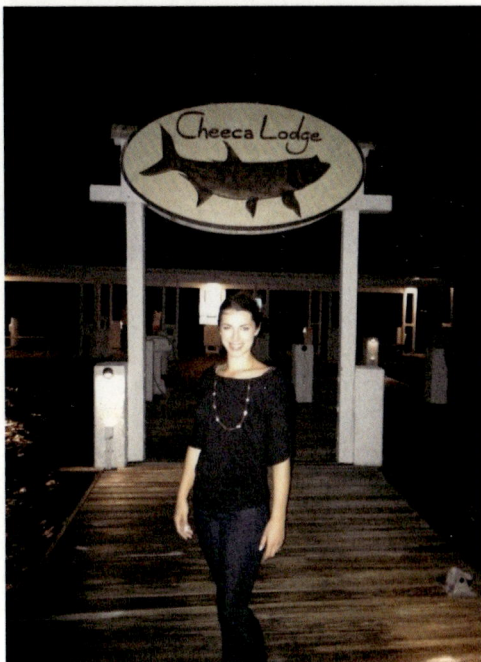

Angela on a recent trip to Cheeca Lodge in the Florida Keys

Just before a reef dive

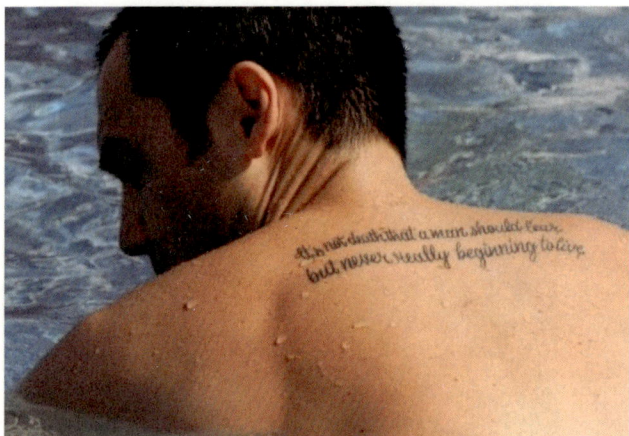

*Oh the irony! This was tattooed on my back prior to the ordeal.
"It's not death that a man should fear, but never really beginning
to live." – Marcus Aurelius*

CHAPTER SEVEN
Where's Your Faith?

Six months.

That was the earliest I could get the surgery. It had to be done by a specialist in London and they were booked solid until July. On the one hand, I suppose that was a reassuring thought: If they're doing so many of these surgeries that they can't schedule my operation for half a year then it mustn't be too dangerous. Right?

That's what I told myself anyway.

I needed some sort of regularity. My life had been utter chaos for the past few weeks, ever since I first felt that damn pulsing in my neck back in Trois-Rivières. Meetings with doctors, shuffling in and out of hospitals, every day it seemed like a new problem reared its head to stress me out even more — not exactly what you want when you've got a serious heart condition.

Less than six months ago, I'd been on top of the world. I'd spent the summer at the Youth Olympics in China and had athletes competing in the World Championships. It was my most successful year yet as a professional coach, and I was ready for a triumphant return to the Elite Canada competition. Instead, I got this… this SVT nightmare.

From the time I opened Revolution with Angela, I'd been passionate about success. Maybe some of that came from my issues with Dad, trying to measure up to his success. There was more to it than just Dad though. There was something inside me bubbling just below the surface like a volcano ready to erupt.

When I was younger, it fueled my competitive drive whenever I went to a gymnastics meet, or a wrestling bout. Then as I got older, it manifested in a passion for growing my business. No matter what I was doing, whether I was thirteen or thirty, I wanted to push myself to succeed.

When it came time to pick the logo for the family businesses, the choice was simple: a charging bull. Strength. Power. Aggression. It captured me and my brand perfectly. I was that charging bull — maybe even a bull in a China shop sometimes. No matter the obstacle, I would face it head-on.

If only I knew then how wrong I was.

In the span of a few short weeks, I went from an unstoppable bull to a terrified man wondering if he might not live to see fifty. My nerves were shot. I needed to get back to my life, to prove I could still be the same man I'd been before I ever heard of SVT.

I jumped headfirst back into my work. If I could just regain control of this small part of my life, then maybe I could pretend that nothing was wrong with me. That petrified shadow of a man dreading a final shot of adenosine, that wasn't me. That was something out of a nightmare. A work of fiction. I was a charging bull. Nothing could hold me back.

Except, something was holding me back. It was a spectre that came to loom over my entire life casting a black shadow over everything I touched. SVT.

In no time at all, I discovered that work was never going to be the same as long as I had this shadow hanging over me. Imagine a high-level gymnastics coach going about his daily routine. He arrives bright and early to the gym, ready to tackle any problems that might arise. He attends to his administrative responsibilities, sorts out some paperwork, and finally, starts to work with a group of top students. Only, he can't. If he does any physical activity, his heart rate might skyrocket, sending him to the hospital or worse. What in the hell should a man like that do?

I hadn't a clue. I couldn't coach. Not really — not at the level I needed to. I could barely walk to my car without thinking about my heart rate. *Am I working too hard? Will it trigger my SVT? What then?*

Who's going to take care of Angela and the kids? The runaway train of my thoughts spiraled endlessly down such winding and treacherous paths.

There was nothing to be gained from worrying about those things. I knew that much, but I had no idea how to stop them from consuming my every waking thought. I had no control over my own mind then. I was a prisoner of my own darkest thoughts.

Soon, even the day-to-day tasks of running a business became nearly impossible. Although I was able to refrain from most physical activities, I couldn't escape the mental stresses that came along with running my own business. People needed to be paid, meetings needed to be booked, emails needed to be answered, finances needed to be tabulated. It all began to pile up, and along with it came stress as I'd never felt before.

If I thought I was stressed before I was diagnosed with SVT, then now I was just about ready to explode. Life doesn't stop just because you get diagnosed with a heart condition; I still had all of my old responsibilities to take care of, only now I had to do all of them without ever raising my heart rate.

If it weren't for Angela, I don't know what I would have done. We had always been partners at Revolution, but now I needed her more than ever. I tried to return to my regular work schedule, and while she didn't protest, she did cover the shifts I missed when I just wasn't able to go to work. More than that, though, she provided emotional support when I needed it most. Whenever I thought I was down and out, she would offer a hand to lift me back up. As the oppressive specter that haunted my life grew to monstrous proportions, at least I had one angel watching over my shoulder, ready to hold me when I faltered.

And falter I did. As the days and weeks dragged on, I sank further into myself, dwelling on my fears, allowing my anxieties to crush my spirit.

Worst of all were the nights. Since I began taking metoprolol to keep my SVT in check, I scarcely slept more than a few hours a night. Difficulty sleeping was listed as one of the potential side effects of the drug, but I didn't think much of it at the start. It was only after a few weeks had passed that the full gravity of my insomnia hit me.

I'm convinced that virtually everyone has experienced some form of insomnia in their lives. Whether to cram for an exam or process a personal loss, most people have pulled the odd all-nighter or two. Maybe you fall into that group too. I know I did before I was diagnosed with SVT. I used to work long hours, and often I lost sleep worrying about this meeting or that deal.

The kind of insomnia I endured post-SVT, though, was an entirely different beast. It was unlike anything I'd ever experienced before, and I pray to God I never experience anything like it again.

At first, I didn't notice much difference. I had a tough time sleeping, sure, but I just attributed that to the metoprolol. The side effects would probably wear off after a few days anyway. Only, they didn't. If anything, they got worse. I could only sleep a few hours each night, and those rare bouts of sleep were always sporadic, interrupted, and restless.

Before SVT, I slept eight or nine hours every night. I was out like a light the minute my head hit the pillow. It actually used to annoy Angela how easy I could get to sleep, just lay down and, snap, unconscious. I slept so deeply I rarely dreamed, at least, not that I remembered.

Nothing could have been further from what I was going through after my diagnosis. Sometimes I would lie awake all night, tossing and turning until my body ached from the effort. Other times I would stay still as a brick and stare at the ceiling as my thoughts raced. Then, when I finally did drift off into an uneasy rest, more often than not I would wake up in the middle of the night drenched in sweat.

The nightmares were like something out of a horror movie, vivid hallucinations that lurched me out of my sleep with explosive force. I don't know if it was the drugs, the anxiety, or some hellish combination of the two, but the result was the same: my life became a waking prison.

Caught between nights tormented by shapeless terrors and days consumed by endless anxiety, I felt any strength that remained in my body shriveling up like a sapling wilting under a scorching sun. I woke each morning feeling exhausted, worked a full-time job during the day, and when I returned home at night, so weak I could barely stand, I still couldn't get any damn sleep.

Day after day, week after week, I could feel myself wasting away. I had never been overly heavy, and less than a month into my six-month wait, I shed more than just excess weight. Between the night sweats and the ever-mounting stress levels, I lost over twenty pounds!

During the waiting period for my operation, I had periodic check-ups with my GP, and I used to tell him about the problems I was dealing with.

"I've lost a ton of weight, I'm not sleeping well, I'm having these crazy nightmares. I don't know what to do, Doc. It's too much.

Too much stress. Too much everything." As I spoke, he nodded attentively. I could feel myself getting worked up, so I took a few deep breaths before continuing.

"It's not just the physical stuff. It's my mind. I can't stop thinking about all the bad shit that might happen to me. What if the surgery doesn't go well? What if it doesn't work, or what if there are complications? What if I... what if I don't make it? What happens then? Who's going to take care of my family? I can't... it's got to go well, that's all there is to it. The surgery has to work. I can't live like this any more. I can't."

Talking about this sort of thing never came easily to me. I liked to deal with things on my own — power through it, and all that — but even I was starting to reach my breaking point. If there was anything this doctor could do to help me get a good night's sleep and relax a bit, then I was willing to listen.

"Are you taking your prescribed medication?" he asked.

"Ya, but I think that's part of the problem," I said. "The pills they gave me, they're messing with my sleep.

My whole body feels completely exhausted and void of energy."

"I understand. That's a common response to the medication, but you still need to take the metoprolol to suppress your SVT. As for your insomnia, I can prescribe some sleeping pills. Those should help regulate your sleep habits."

I left his office with a sense of hope I hadn't felt in ages, and when I got home, I swallowed a sleeping pill, and I had my first proper sleep in I don't know how long. Maybe I could get this thing under control after all. What a sucker I was.

The pills helped in the short term, but at best they were a stopgap. They counteracted some of the side effects of the metoprolol for a time, but they never helped me with the deeper causes of my sleeplessness. The demonic presence of fear and doubt still stalked my every thought, dragging me down to a blackness so deep it threatened to engulf me completely.

Death became an obsession. It was the first thing that crossed my mind in the morning and the last thing I thought of as I finally clawed back a few hours of sleep. Whenever I researched possible outcomes of SVT or the ablation surgery, I lingered on that little word, just five letters but full of so much terror: Death.

Honestly, it surprised me how much that fear of death dominated my life. Growing up, I'd been comfortable with the idea that I was going to die someday. I still remember the first time I saw death up close; it was at my great grandmother's funeral when I was about 8. She had lived to a ripe-old age, had thirteen kids, and enjoyed fairly good health right up until the end. We had an open-casket funeral, and I remember Dad saying to me that I could touch her arm if I wanted to. There was no sorrow, just a celebration of a life well-lived.

Since then, I'd been fortunate enough to avoid losing many people who were close to me. My grandparents had all passed away, and I mourned them at the time, but I was also keenly aware that they had lived full lives. For me, death was sorrow and celebration mixed in equal measure.

That changed in 2011 when I first heard the news: Vladimir Kondratenko was dead.

There have been exactly two people in my life who I thought had this life thing figured out. One was my grandfather, who always seemed to be able to balance work and family without sacrificing either.

Vladi was the other. He taught me more than just how to be a good gymnastics coach; he showed me that it was possible to be a top-notch coach and an amazing person. He was generous, kind, hard-working — the sort of guy everybody loved to be around. Whether you were looking for advice on how to teach gymnastics or you just wanted to talk with someone who knew how to listen, Vladi was the man you'd go to see. He was like a pillar of stone standing still amid the churning sea.

And now he was gone. He was 57 years old.

When I got the phone call telling me that he had passed, my mind went blank. I didn't know how to react. He was sick for a while, so the news wasn't surprising. I'd been visiting with him in the hospital the day before. Still, an emptiness crept into my heart when I heard the news, though it wasn't until a few weeks later that I was able to process what had happened.

I was traveling for a big gymnastics event in Paris, France.

Angela had stayed behind to take care of the kids and the business.

I was alone, and for the first time in my life, I knew the full meaning of the word. I sat in my Paris hotel and cried. For reasons I couldn't understand, Vladi's death hit me with a force unlike any I'd experienced before. Sitting on the bed of my Parisian hotel room, thousands of miles from home, I felt the weight of mourning.

I couldn't believe he was gone. It felt like only yesterday that I'd first met him. I remembered helping him move into his new apartment when he first arrived in Canada. I was there for his first day at the gym. I could still see the broad, toothy grin he flashed whenever one of his pupils landed a perfect movement. Those images were etched in my memory, as clear as could be. He was real, right in front of me, until he wasn't.

All the tired clichés in the world couldn't dam up the tears in my eyes. "He lived a full life and passed away surrounded by friends and family." How many times had I read those words on some obituary sandwiched between the classifieds and the sports section? Now I felt their true hollowness. *Of course, Vladi had been beloved,* I thought to myself, *but now he's gone.*

The funeral. Never in my life have I seen so many people gathered to celebrate one man. They came from all over: old gymnastics friends, pupils, family, many people I recognized and many more I didn't. All of their lives had been touched by this great man. It was a testament to the kind of person he was.

In my youth, I might have taken some consolation from the fact that so many had come to pay their respects and celebrate the life of Vladimir Kondratenko. As it was, all I could think about was the cruel reality of a life cut short. Four years later, as I lay awake in my bed wracked in my latest battle with insomnia, I wondered about what kind of life I've been living and what's really important.

More and more each day, my thoughts turned to that subject, the one thing I wanted to think about least, the one thing I couldn't shake from my mind.

Am I going to die on the operating table? I couldn't control it, my thoughts just returned again and again to the subject. *No,* I thought, *just go to sleep. Don't worry about this now. There's time for that tomorrow.*

This was the battle I fought every night just to try to fall asleep.

Am I going to die from complications? Sleep first. I need sleep. It's 5.23 a.m. now; if I get to sleep by five-thirty, then I can maybe get two hours.

Am I going to die before the operation? I could have an SVT attack any day now. No, don't think like that. Just get some sleep. If I get to sleep now, it's what, 5.45? I can still get an hour and a half.

Am I going to die tomorrow? Today? Who cares — just get some Goddamn sleep! Just an hour. One hour of sleep and I can manage.

Am I going to die?

I don't know, but I've got to go to work in twenty minutes.

Sometimes the skirmish would end in some small victory, a few hours of rest, usually interrupted throughout the night. More often than not, though, I lost the battle against my darkest thoughts, and I would wrestle all night long with visions of death, black as pitch and endless as the night's sky.

Lost in the labyrinth of my own mind, I isolated myself from anyone who might have been able to help. Shortly after my diagnosis, I stopped returning phone calls from friends and family. I didn't want to talk to anybody. I just wanted to be left alone.

Anything seemed better than talking.

The only people who raised me up out of this depression were Angela, Gavin, and Ava. They were my world. Whenever I felt like I couldn't continue or the whole world was weighing down my shoulders, my wife and kids helped raise me up again.

That's why when, three months into the waiting period for my surgery, Angela had to leave for a business trip, my world fell apart.

There was no getting around it. One of us, either Angela or I, had to take one of our top Revolution gymnasts, Sydney Townsend to the world-renowned Jesolo Cup competition in Italy. The girl had been training her butt off to get to this competition and there was no way we could let her down. Since I was in no condition to fly or to deal with jet lag, Angela stepped up. We both agreed it was the best course of action: I would stay home and watch the kids while she would go to the competition. She was only going to be gone a week, so I thought I could manage by myself. How much extra work could it be to see the kids off to school in the morning? The famous last words of fathers the world over.

Adding more work to my daily schedule pushed me from tired and overworked to *Holy shit I need a break. Now.* Between the increased workload and the nervousness I felt from having to take care of Gavin and Ava by myself, I found I was being pushed past my breaking point. There was no way I could function at the level I needed to without finding a way to get some sleep.

The pills the doctor prescribed didn't help matters either. Within a few days of my check-up, I had started to build up a tolerance to the sleeping pills, and after only two weeks, I was taking double the initial dosage — anything I could to dull my fears and claim a precious hour or two of sleep. Worse still, even though I was taking all these pills, my insomnia was intensifying by the day. Each morning, I woke more tired than the next as the cumulative effect of countless restless nights took their toll on my body, yet each night I had a harder and harder time getting to sleep.

By the time Angela left for her trip, I was going days at a time without sleeping. At least once a week, I couldn't sleep at all, no matter how much I tried, no matter how many pills I took. All at once, the mounting pressures in my life came to a head while I was home alone with the kids, and I didn't know how to cope. SVT, metoprolol, fear, anxiety, insomnia, ablation, death: The words swirled endlessly in my mind like an immense whirlpool looking to wash everything away, to crush the life I'd worked so hard to build.

That week, I went three full days without a wink of sleep. My mind was on fire, my body was restless, and there was nothing I could do about it. During the first day, I paced around the house. I tried reading, watching TV, listening to music. Nothing worked. At work, I was a zombie, and at home, I was a wreck. I thought there was no further low to sink to, and then the second day came.

It took all of my remaining strength to get out of bed and crawl in to work. When I got home, the only muscle in my body still functioning was my brain, which continued, against all logic, to race at breakneck speeds. By then, I was too tired to think — no, that's not it. Months of sleep deprivation and constant worry capped off by a 48-hour marathon had leeched any semblance of rhyme or reason to my thoughts, but still, my mind toiled on, imagining waking nightmares as vivid as those in my sleep.

As I rolled on to the third day, my hallucinations degraded into shapeless figures of death, illogical manifestations of my deepest fears. I can't describe to you all the details of that day; I don't remember it well myself. Only snapshots remain, the sight of red streaks running through my eyes as I stared in the mirror, the foggy blackness that crept constantly in the corners of my vision.

Eventually, as the day wore on and I felt my grip on sanity slipping through my fingers, I realized enough was enough. I checked myself into the hospital that afternoon.

They asked me (I don't know who — a doctor I'd never seen before) what was wrong. Fortunately, I still had the presence of mind to answer semi-coherently.

"Sleep. Can't… I need to sleep, but I can't. Haven't slept in…" I counted on my fingers: one, two, "Three days. Think I'm starting to hallucinate. I'm losing my mind. My head, it's… my head's not feeling right. I've got to sleep. Can you give me something to sleep?"

The next thing I knew they were giving me some pills and shuffling me off to one of the hospital beds where, for the first time in days, I lay down and drifted off to sleep.

When I awoke, the doctor told me that my acute episode of insomnia had been caused by the sleeping pills I was taking.

"You should only be taking a maximum of five pills per week," he said. "How many have you taken this week?"

"I'm not sure. I think thirteen, fourteen maybe," I replied. Until I said that out loud, I hadn't realized what a dependency I'd developed.

When I arrived home that evening, I felt more rested than I had in a long time, but my mental state was worse than ever. Not only was I doped up on metoprolol, but apparently now I was reliant on sleeping pills. This coming from a guy who used to avoid taking Advil when he had a headache. I hated pills, but this condition, this damn SVT, was turning me into a different person. What had happened to the confident business owner? Where was the charging bull, ready to face any challenge thrown his way? The man I saw in the mirror was a frightened lamb, too scared of death to take control of his life.

Worst of all, what had happened to the strong, reliable father? I could barely take care of my own kids. Without Angela to carry my slack, the house was falling apart. What kind of father had I turned into? Just the other day, Gavin had fallen asleep watching TV and I couldn't even carry him up the stairs to his room. He was such a little guy, only six years old. He couldn't have weighed more than forty pounds, but I was too weak to lift him up the stairs.

What kind of father was I? A pretty shitty one, I thought. Was this the lasting impression I was going to leave on Gavin and Ava? They were just reaching that age when kids start to form long-term memories, and the first thing they would remember about their dad was that he worried all day and could barely drag himself out of bed in the morning. I hated SVT, but more than that I hated who I'd become.

And I still couldn't fucking sleep.

One night, when my restlessness was particularly bad, I got out of bed and put on a pair of shoes. If I couldn't sleep, I might as well go for a walk. We lived out in the boonies on a long country road, so I figured I would go for a walk to try and tire myself out.

Before I had gone a hundred meters, I felt my heart rate start to rise. *Come on, not now.* I wasn't in SVT yet. This was just the normal beating of a forty-something year-old man going for a brisk walk, but the fear of SVT was perpetually on my mind.

Can't I even walk down to the end of my goddamn driveway without having to worry about SVT? I thought. It was ridiculous. Every step, every breath seemed like it might trigger another attack. *And then what? And then I die?*

All the pent-up frustration, all my anxiety, all my anger, fear, shame, every emotion I'd tried to repress since I was diagnosed began bubbling up. How could I possibly live like that, being afraid to leave the house, to even just walk to my car because of SVT?

The way I was living was no life at all. No life worth living.

I quickened my pace. Screw SVT, fuck death. I was so tired that none of that seemed to matter. *I can't go to sleep. I can't pick up my kid. I can't walk down the road. I'm so messed up.*

I was far from my home now, deep into the country road. There was nobody around except me and a few squeaking bats circling overhead. Nobody around to see the tears streaming down my cheeks or to hear as I started giving voice to thoughts that had long been confined to the silence of my thought.

"I can't live like this," I said. "I don't have the energy to keep on fighting this fight." I stared up at the black night sky. The stars were out, and for the first time since I was a young boy, I saw in them something more than just the twinkling of some far-off sun.

My voice growing stronger the more I spoke, "I need help. I can't go on like this. If this is how it's going to be, just kill me now. God! Just kill me now!"

I spoke the words again, to the God I knew but hadn't talked to in too long. "Just kill me now!"

At that moment, a deadly seriousness filled my voice. I meant what I said. I was a spiritual man, and if

God was out there, I wanted him to hear me. If this was what my life would be like for the next thirty, forty, fifty years, then kill me. I couldn't take any more.

I had tried all my life to do things my own way, to forge my own path, but I couldn't do it any more. I had to put my life in the hands of a greater power, something bigger than myself. That was the only way I could pull myself out of the cavernous pit I'd dug. I had to put my faith in a higher power.

At that moment, standing alone amid the pines and the crisp night air, I really discovered my faith.

That's the first step you need to take if you want to truly overcome your fears and doubts: trust in a power higher than yourself. God and I have had a tumultuous relationship since that first night, but whenever I feel overwhelmed, I know that I can let go and trust in him. For you, the relationship is bound to be different. It is for everybody. What's important is that you are able to believe in something bigger than yourself. If you can do that, if you can admit that there are things you won't ever be able to control, then you can start rebuilding your life to be stronger than you thought possible.

CHAPTER EIGHT
Thinking the Right Thoughts

"Lord, make me chaste — but not yet."

— *Saint Augustine*

It's funny the things that unconsciously pop into your head.

On my way back to the house after my discussion with the big man, this little thought squeaked in through the side door of my mind:

Okay, hang on a second, God. Maybe don't actually kill me now.

I'd been so certain in the moment. Everything was clear to me, as firm and real as the earth beneath my feet or the cool breeze on my cheeks. What happened? I still wanted to change, that much I was still sure about. But something had happened. In a matter of minutes, I was already having doubts, letting negative thoughts creep back, uninvited, into my head.

You've probably experienced it too, or something like it. One day, you're dead set on something. "I'm going to travel around Europe this summer." "I'm going to lose that extra fifteen pounds." "I'm going to stop worrying about the future so much." Then the next day, you're canceling the flight; you've gained ten pounds; you're a bundle of nerves.

Why is that? You're not a bad person. At least, I hope not. And you're not lazy. So why do we fail?

One big part of the problem is those damn unconscious thoughts. It's impossible to change your life if you can't even control your mind.

In the weeks leading up to that fateful midnight walk, I had been engaged in a perpetual war over my own thoughts. That's almost the worst thing about SVT: I knew that worrying about my condition would make it worse but knowing that just made me worry more.

Spotting for one of the gymnasts at work? SVT. Playing a game with the kids? SVT.

Walking into the store to pick up some groceries? SVT. Thinking about SVT? Anxiety, SVT.

It was an endless cycle of self-perpetuating anxiety. No matter what I did, I always ended up returning to that same topic. My brain was like a record playing on an infinite loop: SVT, SVT, are you going to die from SVT? No matter what I tried, I was powerless to change that dreadful tune. In the war for my mind, score one for my subconscious. In fact, score a damn lot for that formidable adversary.

At the time, I thought there was nothing I could do. The mind does what it's going to do and there's nothing you can really do about it. It's just one of those things, like death and taxes. It's just a universal constant:

people have no control over their subconscious minds. That's what I figured.

I couldn't have been more wrong, though I'd need help to see it.

Maybe it's the Brokenshire stubbornness — something I picked up from Dad — or maybe it was the competitive mentality I'd cultivated since I was a kid. I don't know, but whatever the reason, I've always hated accepting help. I want to do things my way. I need to be in control of things, but the worse my condition got, the closer to impossible that became. That was one of the worst things about my SVT. It was so damn uncontrollable. One day I was fine, healthy, strong, and then the next I had this condition. There was no rhyme or reason, no sense to it. I just had it, and there was nothing I could do about it. Worse still, just thinking about it might set off an attack. I'd seen that much in my GP's office. (You'll remember. It was not pleasant.)

I had to hit rock bottom before I was willing to put my faith in a power bigger than myself. The same was true when it came time to take charge of my thoughts, though fortunately this time I didn't end up asking to die, which admittedly was a pleasant change.

I was back in the hospital at the time, recovering from my three-night marathon of insomnia. My first stop was the ER. I already told you about that, but what I didn't tell you was what happened afterwards.

"I need to lie down," I pleaded. "I'm exhausted. Is there anywhere you can put me where I can lie down?"

"Yes," a woman in white scrubs answered, "we have a room. Follow me."

She led me down a sterile white hallway and into a clean, empty room. Empty except for a single neat bed and a door that locked from the outside. Even my sleep-deprived brain could recognize where I was.

This must be where they put the people who've gone off the deep end, I thought groggily. Not exactly the sort of place you want to be when you feel like you're out of your mind.

"Don't be nervous," the woman said. "This is just the only room we have available. I'll leave the door open a crack since it doesn't open from the inside. I'll also turn the light off for you."

"Thanks."

"One last thing. There's a specialist on call tonight who works with people struggling with sleep and thought. Would it be all right with you if I sent her down to talk with you?"

"Yes, please."

And just like that, I was alone in the dark. Eyes shut. Lying down. Wide fucking awake.

I don't know how long I lay there, sometimes with my eyes clamped shut and other times staring into the blackness of the walls. I felt like I was about to go crazy when the door opened wide and a fit, middle-aged woman entered the room.

She looked around my age, maybe a bit older, with blonde, curly, shoulder-length hair.

"You must be Aaron," she said. There was a warmth to her voice that seemed to match the smile on her face. "My name is Suzanne. I'm the sleep expert at this hospital. Well, not 'at this hospital' really. I run a clinic in the area, and I sometimes come into the hospital to lend a hand. And not really a 'sleep expert'. More like a thoughts expert."

"A thoughts expert?" I said, sitting up on the end of the bed. "What do you mean?"

"I help people understand and control their thoughts, eliminating the negative and strengthening the positive. Cognitive behavioural therapy, if you want to get technical about it."

"And that can help me sleep?"

"That's one of the benefits, sure. But there's a lot more to it than that. Cognitive thought is a comprehensive process with a host of positive outcomes, both physical and psychological."

There must have been something in my face that gave away my skepticism.

"Don't believe me?" she asked. "I know, it can sound like a whole lot of mumbo-jumbo at first like I'm just going to tell you that 'through the power of positive thinking, you can cure all your problems,' but cognitive thought isn't like that. What I do has been clinically proven to be equally as effective as medication for treating a range of issues from insomnia to depression and even post-traumatic stress disorder."

"As long as it helps me sleep." At that point, I was willing to give anything a shot as long as it promised to help me sleep. "I've been awake for three days. Please, I'm desperate."

"I understand," she said in a low voice, and I believed her. She sat on the bed beside me. Her blue eyes pierced through my skull and into my soul.

"I went through the same thing after my divorce. It was like my entire world was turned upside down in an instant. Everything I had thought was stable and constant got ripped from their foundations. One minute, I was happily married, and the next, I was alone. Just like that.

"After my husband left, I was a wreck. I didn't want to go out; I didn't want to go to work. I didn't want to do anything. Everything just seemed to remind me of my husband, and whenever I thought about him, those horrible feelings came racing to the surface. I was depressed, furious, lonely, inconsolable. I wanted to scream at him; I wanted to be loved by him; I wanted everything to go back to how it was before this nightmare ever happened.

"For three months, I barely slept a wink. Everywhere I looked, I saw bitter reminders of the life I used to lead. A cast-iron pan that had been a wedding gift. The navy-blue walls that he had protested so vigorously against painting. A trinket here, a bobble there, always something that would call to mind some fond memory. I would stay awake all night thinking

127

about our past or worrying about my future. What could I have done differently? What was I going to do now? Who gets what in the divorce? How could I start dating again after fifteen years of marriage? An endless stream of questions bombarding my mind, causing me stress, preventing me from sleeping.

"I understand, Aaron. The doctors told me about what you've been going through. I went through it too, and I came out the other side. There was one low point where I barely slept for two weeks. I'm here to tell you that you're not alone. You are not alone. You have your family, your doctors, and me if you want my help. Do you want my help?"

I looked up at her with tears streaming down my face. To this day, I have no idea when I began to cry, but something she had said profoundly touched me. Just knowing that the woman sitting beside me had gone through the same sort of problems I was experiencing meant the world to me. If you only take one message away from this book, that might be that you're not alone in your struggle and there is hope.

I was not alone, and neither are you. No matter how dark the path looks, no matter how many setbacks you face along the way, you can make it through. Even when you're all alone, even if it seems like no one understands what you're dealing with, know that there are people out there who can relate to what you're going through. Take it from me, a guy who only learned that lesson after three days of terrifying insomnia and a trip to the ER. You are never as alone as you think you are.

But I still had to answer her question.

"Yes," I said. There was nothing left to say. "Yes. Please help me."

A week later, I met Suzanne at her practice. It was just across the road from the hospital in a small, unassuming building. I entered and waited in the reception area for my scheduled appointment.

Ever since our first meeting, I'd felt like a great burden had been eased from my shoulders and I couldn't wait to pick up where we left off.

"Ms O'Neil will see you now," the receptionist said. O'Neil. In my excitement, I'd forgotten to ask her last name at the hospital.

I entered her office and took a seat in an open chair opposite her desk.

"How have you been?" Suzanne asked.

"Much better. Just talking about these things is really helpful," I said.

"I'm glad," she said, a slight smile appearing on the corners of her lips. Even those sorts of daily expressions sounded genuine coming from her. "Today, I just want to introduce you to the basics of cognitive thought."

"You mentioned that term at the hospital, but I still don't really know what it means," I said.

"Don't worry. It sounds more complicated than it is. In short, cognitive thought is a method of understanding how we think about things and how we can control what we think."

"Ya, you're gonna have to run that by me again."

"First, let me ask you a question. Who taught you how to tie your shoelaces?"

"My mom, I guess."

"And who taught you to drive a car?"

"Definitely my dad."

"OK, and who taught you how to think?"

I was silent.

"Exactly," she said. "Nobody teaches you how to think; you just do it. Yet just like tying our shoelaces or driving a car, there is a right way and a wrong way to think — or more accurately a healthy and an unhealthy way to think. There is a protocol out there for mental well-being, a method of thought deflection that minimizes negative thoughts and maximizes positive ones: That is what I mean by cognitive thought.

"First, you have to be able to acknowledge what you're thinking about in any given moment. What might you be thinking about that keeps you from getting to sleep?"

"Death," I answered without hesitation.

She nodded solemnly. "That's a common one, unfortunately. You would start by acknowledging the thought. Maybe for you, it's something like this: 'I'm afraid I'm going to die because of my heart.' That's your physical condition, right? SVT?"

I nodded. I'd sent her some additional information about my case in advance of our meeting.

"Okay. Then, once you've acknowledged the thought, ask yourself whether that's something positive or negative. Is that thought working for you or against you? Is it really worth worrying about this possible complication or that? Should you really be working yourself into a tizzy doing all sorts of research on the internet of all the possible complications associated with your surgery, staying up until three in the morning worrying about death? What are you really accomplishing? Nothing. Are those thoughts really helping you get where you want to go? Are they helping you live a good life? Get sleep? No."

"As soon as you've acknowledged a thought that's detrimental, that's faulty, that's flawed, that's negative, you have to stop yourself right there. You have to replace that thought with another one. You have to choose another thought, an opposite one. To do that, you have to employ tactics. Oppositional thinking is one of them. So, you're worried about death. It happens to all of us from time to time. What's an oppositional thought you could think of to replace that worry?"

"I'm not really sure. Maybe I could think about my kids?"

"That's a start. You've moved the focus away from death.

"However, that's still not quite oppositional thinking. For real oppositional thinking, you need to be even more direct. Just take the exact opposite of whatever you're thinking and focus on that. One more time, what are you afraid of?"

"I'm afraid I'm going to have an SVT attack and die."

"Okay, now think the exact opposite of that."

"So, I would just think, 'I'm not going to die'?"

"Now you're getting it. 'I'm not going to die. I'm healthy, I'm happy; I'm going to live to be a hundred.'"

"But isn't that just denial?" I asked. "I would only be running away from reality. Shouldn't I face tough truths head-on?"

"Has that approach been working for you?" She let the question stew for a while. She knew the answer as well as I did.

"I understand your concern," she continued. "Sometimes we feel like we need to be tough and confront our problems directly. Especially with my male clients, using tactics like oppositional thinking can feel like a retreat. Nothing could be further from the truth though. What's more important: living a happy, healthy, well-adjusted life, or burying our pain under a tough exterior?"

"Cognitive thought and oppositional thinking are just two tools we can use to help shape our minds in a productive way," she said. "It doesn't really matter whether or not your oppositional thoughts are one hundred percent literally true. What matters is they help you to live your best life, whatever that means to you.

Imagine you *do* live to be a hundred years old. You're forty-two now, right? Do you want to look back and think to yourself, 'Wow, I spent years forty-two to one hundred just worrying about dying'? Why waste all that time, all that effort, all those sleepless, panicked nights when you didn't have to?"

"I... I hadn't thought about it like that before."

"That's perfectly understandable. I remember when I first started thinking cognitively after my divorce. It was a shock, but the more you practice, the easier it becomes. Do you play any sports, Aaron?"

"Ya, you could say that," I said.

"Well, isn't it the same with sports? The movements might seem difficult, uncomfortable at first, but the more you practice them, the easier they become until eventually, they're as natural as breathing. You can reach that stage with cognitive thinking too; it becomes almost second nature. At that point, you can think of cognitive thought almost like a mental ninja. It sits on your shoulder and waits, and whenever a flawed, negative thought appears, it swats it out of the air before it can get to you. Then you replace that thought with a positive one: that's oppositional thinking. Is this starting to make any sense at all?"

It more than made sense. It opened my eyes to an entirely new way of viewing the world around me and my place in it. For years, decades, I'd been harbouring negative thoughts. Insomnia was only the latest manifestation of a much deeper problem. I had never before stopped to analyze the way I was thinking, to consider whether my obsessive, competitive mentality was helping or hurting me.

Who was I helping when I beat myself up for losing that wrestling match or falling during my gymnastics meet? When I pushed myself time and time again to try and prove myself to Dad, what good was that doing? I became so focused on dominating, on becoming that charging Brokenshire bull, that I'd lost all sense of perspective. Was that really how I wanted to live my life?

SVT might have been the physical condition that put me in the hospital, but my mental health was due for an overhaul too. I needed to slow down, to take a moment to stop and ask myself: are these thoughts helping me or hurting me?

I left Suzanne's office with a whole new perspective on my condition. For the first time since my whole SVT nightmare began, I felt like there was something I could do about it. Cognitive thought had armed me with the tools to start turning my life around. There would be more hardships ahead, of that I was sure, but for the first time since my diagnosis, I held hope for the future. Not only could I survive, but I could actually come out the other side stronger than ever before.

Thought and faith became the pillars around which I gathered the fragments of my life, but they were only the beginning. The journey I was embarking on expanded until it encompassed all aspects of my life, the physical, the mental, and the spiritual. To become the best I could be, I had to achieve a unified balance of body and mind, something I'd never even attempted before.

The road before me was long, longer than I'd ever imagined, but equipped with lessons contained in this book, I knew that I was ready for any challenges that came my way.

The key is to keep company only with people who uplift you, whose presence calls forth your best.

— *Epictetus*

CHAPTER NINE
The Deepest of Sleeps

In the week after that first meeting with Suzanne, my whole life started to change.

At first, it was just small things, but isn't that always how it is? You don't just wake up one day with the life you always wanted. You have to work for it. That's something I always thought I had understood when I was younger. If you want to be successful, you have to put in the hours, whether that's in the gym or the office.

That's what I thought, and I wasn't entirely wrong. Success, health, happiness; these aren't things that just happen overnight. They're things that you have to build up gradually, slowly, sometimes over the course of a lifetime. What I didn't realize when I was working out like a mad man for the next gymnastics meet or putting in sixty-hour weeks at my business, was that overworking is just as bad, if not worse, than slacking off.

If the road to success is paved, brick by brick, with a thousand daily efforts, then so too is the path to failure. Both happen so gradually that they tend to sneak up on you. One day, you're going about life, as usual, making sure you follow healthy, positive habits, taking care of your kids and letting your wife know how much you appreciate her, eating right, sleeping well, and suddenly you realize that you've built yourself a nice little life. There are no trumpets or applause, just a deep feeling of contentment and a profound sense of relaxation.

Likewise, if you're going about your life as usual and you chose to follow unhealthy habits, then the reverse happens. You find yourself spending more time crunching the quarterly budget than you do watching your kids play soccer in the yard. You grab a Big Mac on the way to work instead of sitting down to eat dinner with your family. You work overtime this week so you can have time off next week, then next week something comes up and you have to stay late again. Next week, you say, but even you're beginning to doubt your own promises.

You stress over all the details, you work your ass off to be the best version of yourself you can be, and before you know it, you're lying on the cold floor of some Godforsaken gymnasium wondering if your heart will ever slow down. Trust me, before you know it, your life is crumbling around you and you're sinking into a pit you can't see any way out of. They might just seem like small things at first, but if you don't start correcting those small things, then soon you'll discover just how fast a trickle of pebbles can start an avalanche.

Armed with the tools I learned from my cognitive thought sessions, I was already starting to see some of those small things turn from negatives into positives.

Right away, I had more energy. I never realized how much my stress and anxiety had been sapping my mental strength. All the time I'd spent wrestling with my darkest thoughts had taken its toll without me even realizing it. Now that I had my negative emotions somewhat under control — I won't say eliminated since I'm still on the path of improving my thoughts — it felt like a cool wave had washed over me, taking with it years of fear and doubt.

While I was slowly starting to catch negative thoughts through cognitive thinking, I also noticed subtle improvements in my spiritual life. Now, I'm not here to tell you which church you should go to or which God(s) you should believe in. Faith is bigger than that. Faith means acknowledging that you can't do this on your own. Faith means finding your centre, something you can hold onto when the world around you seems to be spiraling out of control.

And that's exactly what I did. With my family by my side, I found a way to survive the craziness that had nearly swallowed me up in the months that I waited for my surgery. I never would have thought it was possible during that low time, but I could actually see the light at the end of this seemingly endless tunnel.

The past few weeks were beginning to feel like just one long, horrible nightmare, one I was immeasurably happy to awaken from.

Then, I felt something that I feared I'd lost forever. I started to feel almost normal.

Normal. I never thought I'd live to see the day that I would give an arm and a leg just to feel normal.

But I promised you something more than that. I told you that this would be the story of how I rebuilt my life stronger than ever after my diagnosis. I promised that I would show you how I finally answered the unspoken question that had dogged me my entire life, that I would answer the question: "How Good Could You Be?"

Faith and thought helped pull me out of my despair, but to take that next step, to be as good as I could be, I needed to take more concrete actions. I worked by trial and error, testing this technique and that method, taking this advice and experimenting with that diet. In the remaining months before my surgery, I can't count how many different changes I had made to my life, some helpful and some not so helpful; some life-changing discoveries.

That's why I decided to write this book. When I was at rock bottom, asking God to just kill me now if my life was going to keep going the way it had been, I realized I had to make some drastic changes. I knew from the depths of my soul that something needed to change — the only problem was I didn't know exactly what.

Take it from me. If you want to improve not only your mind but also your body, then you've got to be willing to ask for help, and I have learned to rely on all sorts of people.

I wouldn't be here today without my family, without Angela, Gavin, and Ava, who motivate me every day to live a better, healthier, more balanced life; without my mom, whose advice and loving support helped me through some of my darkest times; without my siblings, Greg and Leah; and of course, without Dad. For years — decades, really — I struggled to live up to his expectations. However, without the lessons he taught me and the values he instilled in me, I wouldn't be who I am today.

Each and every one of those people, and many, many more who helped along my way — Lawson, Elvira, Vladi, Suzanne, all the doctors, EMS, and medical staff who made my recovery possible — were indispensable in saving me, shaping who I had become and who I was going to be moving forward. They were my friends, my mentors, my teachers, my guides and my saviours.

Let me be some support for you. Let me guide you through the steps you need to take to be the best you can be. Let me help you to discover the life you never thought you were capable of. Let me show you how good you can be!

There are four major areas of my life that I worked to improve in the lead-up to my surgery: sleep, diet, exercise, and thought. I can't tell you which to focus on first. They aren't steps you follow one after another. Rather, each is like a leg of a sturdy table. They work in tandem, and if you remove one, the whole table collapses. Likewise, should one leg be shorter or less sturdy than the others, then the table might not collapse, but instead, the balance suffers.

For me, sleep was an obvious area of my life that needed to be addressed immediately. While I consciously worked on improving all four aspects at the same time, it's difficult to improve your diet, for example, when you're only getting an hour of sleep a night.

I had been set on the path to a healthier sleep by my introduction to cognitive thought, but there was much more work to be done than simply a few mental exercises, no matter how revolutionary those exercises were to me.

"There's got to be something more I can do," I mused aloud one night after dinner. I hadn't really anticipated response, but Angela, sensing my irritation, spoke from across the table.

"Isn't the cognitive whatever working?" she asked.

"Ya, it's like night and day," I said. "My stress is way down, my energy's up. It's like I've taken back control of my life — at least, part of it."

"Then why do you keep tossing and turning all night? I'm still sore from where you elbowed me last night," she said with a smirk.

"I don't know. That's the problem. I just don't know what's going on, or what my problem even is. Other than the fact that I can't sleep, obviously."

"Obviously," she said, echoing my tone precisely. Then, her large, brown eyes turning suddenly serious, she crinkled her eyebrows and a deep look of thoughtfulness swept over her face. "That is a conundrum. How to solve a problem when you're not really sure what the problem is."

There was a long silence between us before she spoke again.

"Well, what would you tell a gymnast if she had a problem that she didn't know how to fix?"

"That's easy," I said. "I would tell her to listen to a good coach. But there aren't any coaches for sleeping."

"Really? Have you actually tried looking?"

Sheepishly, I admitted that I hadn't. At least, not really.

Sometimes in the dead of night when my insomnia was particularly bad, I would do a bit of online research, but there's a world of difference between the incoherent, sleep-deprived Google searches of a desperate man and real, intelligent research.

That night, I spent three hours glued to my laptop screen learning everything I possibly could about improving one's sleep habits. Then the next night, more of the same. And again, and again, until I knew all there was to know about sleeping habits.

This was different from my previous forays into online research though. When I was first diagnosed with SVT, for example, I fell down an endless rabbit hole of opinions from online medical 'experts' and started obsessing over every worst-case outcome. Without proper direction, the same obsessive personality that has served me well in sports and business can turn me into my own worst enemy.

This time I was determined to focus my energy positively. By approaching the task with a different state of mind, one more focused on finding solutions than dwelling on problems, I was able to avoid the pitfalls I'd fallen into earlier. I became an information sponge, and the more I learned, the more I saw that there were real, practical things I could be doing to improve my sleep patterns, sort of like best practices for sleep — sleep hygiene, I learned it was called.

The first thing I learned about were the optimal conditions you should try to create in your room. Below 68 degrees Fahrenheit is ideal and dark. Like, pitch black. No lamps. No TVs. Definitely no cell phones. Just a cool, completely dark room with nothing to distract you from getting a good night's sleep.

That might seem like simple advice, but in practice, it's much more difficult than you might expect. People have become reliant on the distraction of technology, and I'm no exception. At first, it was difficult to put the phone down and turn off the TV, but you know what's more difficult? Trying to work a full-time job and raise two young kids on less than an hour of sleep a night.

I found that I just had to quit cold turkey. I took the TV out of my room and started to leave my phone charging in another room. No phone or TV for at least two hours before bed. Simple.

Once I had my room set up just the way I wanted it, I turned my attention to some behavioural issues that might be affecting my sleep. I began by cutting out any snacking or exercising after eight p.m. Your body should be winding down to sleep, not getting pumped up. If you eat something just before going to bed, what do you think your body is going to be doing all night? While your mind is fast asleep trying to get some rest, your body is working overtime trying to digest the food you just ate.

After that, I began incorporating some positive behaviours to actively encourage a healthier sleep. I started by just doing some basic stretches to loosen up my body and relax after a long day of work. Even just a light routine of stretching can help tremendously with the quality of your sleep.

Soon, I was incorporating more advanced techniques into my repertoire. Within a week or two of my initial research into sleep hygiene, I was meditating before going to sleep and utilizing more nuanced muscle relaxation exercises, including doing yoga during the day. I won't go into too much detail here, though, since everyone needs to find a routine that works for them.

Found a certain type of stretch that helps you relax? Do it.

Discovered a type of meditation that clears your mind at night? Go for it. Each person's sleep hygiene is unique. Find aspects and steps that work for you and stick to them.

Consistency is one of the most important principles to keep in mind when regulating your sleep. Find a consistent bedtime and wake-up time, including weekends, that allows you to get as much sleep as you need and then stick to it. I find that I need eight hours to function at an optimal level, so I devised a schedule that allowed me to get that much sleep.

You should be treating sleep with the same seriousness you would any other major dimension of health, including diet and exercise. If you approach it with that sort of mindset, then you'll experience results just like you would with your diet and exercise. I for one found that the more effort I put into creating a consistent schedule and an actionable plan ahead of time, the better sleep I got.

In the end, sleep hygiene is an individual practice. There will be certain things that I find beneficial that other people may find not as helpful. Still, I encourage you to try these practices and focus in on the ones that work for you:

- Try using an eye mask and/or earplugs. They work to block the senses that can keep you awake.
- Don't over-hydrate before bed. There's nothing worse than feeling the sweet approach of a blissful sleep only to be interrupted because you have to, well, I don't think I need to explain this one.
- Restrict or eliminate your alcohol, chocolate, sugar, and caffeine intake during the day. It should go without saying, but don't drink a cup of coffee within a few hours of trying to get to sleep. The effects of caffeine last longer than you might think.
- Try to participate in regular exercise during the day. I'll have more to say about this in the next chapter.
- Make sure that any medications you're taking aren't interfering with your sleep. If you have any concerns about the medication you're taking, talk to your doctor.
- No naps after four p.m. Taking late naps makes it more difficult to get to sleep at night.
- Make sure your bed is as comfortable as possible and suits your preferences.
- Form a relaxing ritual which you practice each night. Like reading? Read a chapter each night before settling down. Enjoy warm baths? Go right ahead.

The purpose of this list is to provide suggestions for getting a good night's sleep. In the end, you need to find sleep hygiene that works for you and allows you to thrive. Only by doing so can you truly realize this first leg of the balanced life. Only by mastering sleep can you move one step closer to becoming the person you always dreamed you could be.

CHAPTER TEN
Health

Hang on to your youthful enthusiasms — you'll be
able to use them better when you're older.

— Seneca

By now you're probably wondering: OK, thoughts,
sleep. That's awesome! But what do I need to do
physically to be the best version of myself?

Exercise, athletics, physical health — they've been
a huge part of my life for as long as I can remember.
From my early days of roughhousing with my brother
in the fields and forests to my obsession with sports and
competition, I've always been a relatively fit guy. It's
important to me, and I like to think I ended up making a
pretty good career out of it. As a gymnastics coach, I
advocate every day for physical health just as much as
the mental aspect of health.

That being said, even though you know the right
thing to do doesn't mean you're always going to do it.
Especially when you're as stubborn as I am.

Immediately after my diagnosis, I was terrified of
any sort of physical exertion. Walking to my car,

climbing a flight of stairs, any sort of exercise at all set off fears of another attack, but as the weeks dragged on without incident, I started to feel my confidence returning. I hadn't dropped dead yet, so I must be doing something right.

Around the same time, I was still struggling with insomnia on a nightly basis. I hadn't met Suzanne or started practicing cognitive thought. I was just a bundle of frayed nerves, always on edge, never quite sure what to do next.

At that point, all I knew was that I couldn't keep doing what I was doing. That much seemed obvious. There was something seriously wrong with me, something more than just SVT, though I didn't understand it at the time. I remained so fixated on my physical conditions — the SVT, the drugs, insomnia — that everything else just seemed insignificant, like the dull hum of traffic on a busy street, something faintly noticed but never really paid attention to.

And so I started pacing, searching for answers to questions I didn't even know how to ask. That's what I did whenever I couldn't sleep. I walked.

I used to walk down our road practically every day and night, especially when my insomnia was bad. I knew that walking was good for you, so whenever I couldn't sleep, instead of staring at the clock in my room as the glowing numbers flashed: 3.00 a.m.; 4.00 a.m.; 5.00 a.m. I started walking.

We lived on a remote country road, so at night there weren't any cars on the road. It was just me, the stars, and the occasional cricket. Nothing to distract me, give me anxiety, cause me stress. Just a walk down the road to burn off restless energy and get those good endorphins flowing that I'd heard so much about.

It sounded good in theory, so I began a daily ritual in which I walked down the road until I reached a road sign. I'd touch the sign, then head back to my house. I figure it must have been a bit over a kilometer to the sign, so I measured the distance. Eleven minutes to the sign, then eleven minutes back. I liked the symmetry of it — it helped me establish a daily routine. I walked to the sign and back twice a day, usually once during the day and once at night. It helped return the structure to my life and allowed me to exercise in a healthy way.

Then I overdid it.

All the research I did said that walking was good for you, and I was up all night anyway, so I took to longer and longer nighttime walks. I would walk to the sign and back once, then twice, then three times, then more times than I want to count. If I couldn't sleep, I might as well be doing something productive.

Except it verged on false productivity. I was filling the time in any way I could without addressing the underlying problems. It was over-trying working hard, not working smart.

It was the same way with my diet. I remember hearing a supposed expert saying that you should drink about eight large glasses of water a day. So, I tried that. I was drinking eight glasses a day plus all the hydration provided in my food. And what effect did it have on me? The difference I noticed was that I was pissing every five minutes. Eventually, it became clear to me that I was overdoing it.

That's the type of person I am, and maybe you are too.

When I try something, I want to be very good at it. I want to master every little thing I try, to push myself further, to do everything the best I possibly can. It can be a great tool, that fiery ambition, but it can also be a pitfall on the road to true success.

Everything is fine when your drive pushes you to achieve greatness in athletics, business, whatever it is that you're passionate about. But sometimes passion without contemplation, ambition without balance, can destroy you. Or at least leave you running to the bathroom twenty times a day.

After I improved my way of thinking through cognitive thought and started to achieve a better balance in my life, I returned to improving my fitness. I started walking again. By my rough math, I figure I must have walked over 2,000 kilometers down that quiet road in front of my house. I would walk until my legs burned and I could feel the strength returning to my muscles. I was never going to be that weak again. I was never going to be too tired to play with my kids. I was going to be stronger, even better than I'd been before my diagnosis.

As the weeks wore on, my legs were getting more sore by the day, but I knew I was getting healthier too. I didn't want to stop exercising, not when it felt like I was just starting to take my life back. I needed something I could do that would give my legs a rest but also keep my momentum moving forward.

That's when I took up swimming.

It had been over three decades since my parents first tried to enroll me in swimming as a kid, it didn't go so well then. Of course, in the meantime, I'd learned to swim decently well, but it had never been one of my athletic passions. Until now.

When I was in the pool, it was like I'd slipped into another world. The solitude was captivating, and as I sliced my way through the crystal-clear water, I was utterly alone with only my new, positive thoughts for company. A month earlier and that prospect would have terrified me, but with the work I'd put into improving my mentality, I now relished the chance to escape the hustle and bustle of the busy world and disappear into the weightless world just beneath the surface of the pool.

I swam all through the winter and into the spring while waiting for my surgery. Then, as the hot summer days swept away the last remnants of cold and the stunning Ontario landscape revealed itself in all its glory, a thought occurred to me that seemed at first obvious and later profound: why aren't I taking advantage of this opportunity? There was so much beauty all around me in my natural surroundings, yet I had never seen it before — not fully, anyway.

So together with my regular swimming and walking schedule, I decided to take up cycling.

I started out simple, just biking around our country roads, a few kilometers here or there, nothing too serious, but soon I progressed to longer and longer rides.

If swimming had given me another world to escape to, then cycling broke down any barriers that remained. When I was out biking, feeling the heat of the sun on my bare back and the wind sweeping across my brow, I was free. There was no SVT, no looming heart surgery, no stress or anxiety, flying away from fear and doubt and towards — who knows what? The world was open to me for the first time in a long time and I was excited to see what the future would bring.

Then my wife, Angela, had a brilliant idea.

"You're getting pretty serious about this cycling," she said after I returned from my latest outing.

"Yes! It's so fun. I'm loving it"

"And you've been swimming like a dolphin for the past few months too."

"It's fantastic exercise. I haven't felt this good in years."

"It's like you are training for a triathlon!"

The words hung in the air for several seconds before either of us spoke again. I had never thought about that before. It just seemed so out of my reach. I couldn't complete a triathlon. People with heart conditions don't do triathlons.

"Of course, you'd have to do it sometime after the surgery, but you've already got two-thirds of it down. All you'd have to do is take up running. Something to think about, I guess," she said.

I did, and the more I thought about it, the more realistic it seemed. I wasn't actively training with a serious goal in mind, not by a long shot. I still didn't know the limits I could push my body to, and I didn't want to mess anything up before the surgery, but in the back of my mind, a vision started coalescing.

Why not? Why not do this difficult, insane, ridiculous thing?

Why not, if I want to push myself to be better than I ever thought possible, to become the person I always knew I could become? I started doing some research and discovered that there were several other people with SVT who had gone on to run marathons and triathlons. Why not me too?

I knew it wouldn't be easy, but that was part of the reason I wanted to do it. A big reason, actually. I've never been one to take the easy path. It wasn't easy competing in high-level gymnastics or wrestling, but I did it. It wasn't easy doing a career 180 from real estate to coaching, but I did that too. And it wasn't easy opening a new gym, just Angela and I, but we did it.

Dreams of triathlon splendour would have to wait, though, until after my surgery. I incorporated a bit of light jogging into my routine, but I was careful not to overdo it. I wanted desperately to improve myself, but I couldn't risk my health in doing so. My surgery was rapidly approaching, and I had to focus on that. If I got the all-clear from the doctor after — *when* I got the all-clear — then maybe I could start training more seriously for the next stage of my life. But if I've learned anything from this whole SVT experience, it's that you shouldn't dwell on the future; you never know what twists might come your way before then.

Still, as the day of my surgery drew near, I couldn't believe how different I felt from when I first got the news of my SVT. In less than a week, a doctor was going to poke a hole in my leg, send an instrument all the way up to my core, and burn away a node on my heart. And I felt fine.

In anticipation of the surgery, we decided to rent a cottage and spend the week relaxing, just me, Angela, Gavin, Ava, along with a close friend of mine, Kelly Manjak, and his sons. Kelly was, and still is, one of the best gymnastics coaches in the world, having coached Olympic Gold Medalist, Kyle Shewfelt. Having great people like Kelly around in my life, both professionally as well as personally, helped me stay grounded, so I was thrilled that he was around in the lead-up to my surgery.

When we got to the cottage, the weather was wonderful: clear skies, warm breeze, the smell of fresh pines and smouldering campfires wafting over the rustic property. Big enough for the group of us, but not so big you'd forget you were at a cottage. The building itself faced out over a broad, clear lake, and at the end of a small gravel path leading down to the water's edge sat a small wooden dock.

For the next few days, I soaked up the sun and enjoyed some long-overdue time away from work, but I also kept up with my exercise. Each morning, I'd go for a short, slow jog, followed by a cycle around the lake or a swim along the shoreline — sometimes both. Angela and the kids were having a great time, and everything was going off without a hitch. Until it wasn't. You see... I had to come off the metoprolol the week before my surgery.

I first noticed it when I was sitting with my feet dangling over the edge of the dock after a swim. I'd just been for a bike ride and hopped in the water to cool off, but something was wrong. It was almost imperceptible at first, but it soon grew to an unmistakable pounding. That same pulsating feeling at the base of my neck, the accelerating *thump-thump* that I thought I'd never experience again. I was having an SVT attack!

Sprawled on my back, I gasped for air with the hunger of a drowning animal. This was bad, as bad as the one that sent me to the hospital.

"Are you alright?" Kelly asked. He'd been sitting on the dock with Angela and me, hoping to pass the time soaking up a few rays before heading back from the cottage. I knew from the tone of his voice he wasn't expecting anything like this.

"SVT," I said, stuttering between the letters. It was all I could choke out before my head started spinning.

"Shit," he said, "is there anything I can do?"

I shook my head. My doctors said I had to wean myself off the meds in the week before the surgery, so I'd been cutting my doses for the past few weeks. By now, I was totally drug-free. If I took any pills then, it would have interfered with the surgery, the doctors would call it off and I'd have to wait another six months. I couldn't wait another six months. I had no other options: I had to weather this storm.

"Help me get him on his feet," Angela said. "Aaron, we're going to take you back to the cottage and you can just lie down, relax, breathe. Remember, as the doctor told you."

The last time we visited the hospital, the doctor had told me about some basic methods to try and subside an SVT attack. Some people try shocking themselves out of it with cold water. Others try coughing, and others try breathing exercises. None of those had ever really helped me before, but they couldn't hurt. I would try just about anything then.

As I hobbled my way back to the cottage and then lay flat on my back staring at the ceiling, I couldn't help thinking to myself how stupid I'd been. *One week until your surgery, one week off the meds, and you can't take a break from training for a fucking triathlon? You must be out of your mind!*

I'd done it again, and it wouldn't be the last time. I pushed myself too far, worked hard not smart, and now I was paying the price. The flashing number on my heart rate monitor was a harsh reminder of my over-ambitiousness: 242.

Two hundred and forty-two heartbeats per minute. It might as well have read 242 days you'll have to wait for another surgery; 242 laps in the pool you didn't need to do; 242 amazing experiences you're going to miss if you screw this up.

But I couldn't think like that. That was panic. That was what made SVT attacks worse. I had to calm myself, focus on my breathing, and tell myself that everything was going to work out. *I am going to be healthy. I was the healthiest person in the world. I am fine, I am calm, this attack is ending, I feel good.* I cognitively reassured myself.

Then, after five minutes, which felt more like five hours, it stopped. That might not seem long considering some of my longest attacks lasted forty minutes or more, but trust me, it was long enough.

"I'm all right now," I said, grabbing Kelly's outstretched hand and pulling myself to a seated position.

"Jesus, you really scared me," he replied, though he didn't have to. His pale face told the whole story.

Luckily, the kids weren't around. It was just Kelly, Angela, and me. Kelly sat in a plain wooden chair while Angela sat beside me on the couch like a sick child.

Kelly continued, "I knew you had this condition. I knew about it, but I didn't understand. Now I think I do. I can see how hard this is on you... how hard it is on your family. I can see how devastating it is for you, both of you." Angela and I both nodded mutely.

That's the way Kelly is, very reflective, philosophical. He cuts to the heart of the matter, and in that moment, none of us had anything else to say.

It was time. The months of waiting. Insomnia. The anxiety. The fear. That was all in the past. It had all come to this. Sitting in the waiting room of the University Hospital in London, Ontario, I took a deep breath. In less than an hour, a doctor was going to perform heart surgery and I would know once and for all whether I was going to be free from this monster, SVT, or not. Even now I can't quite describe the sensation. Something like a mixture of dread and anticipation, a longing to get it over with and a terrible sense of foreboding: terror, relief, excitement, disbelief, all churning together in one potent concoction.

As I came into full consciousness post-surgery. Angela and my dad came clearly into view. I was alive! It didn't seem real. But it was real, just as real as the delicate hand of my wife clasped on top of my own fingers.

This was it. It was time to find out my fate. The surgeon entered the room…

"You're good."

Two simple words and my life was changing in the most positive and exciting way possible! Dispersing the all-consuming cloud that had hovered over my life these past six months.

The room, which had been deathly silent until then, seemed to let out a collective exhale. It had been several hours since the surgery. I didn't die, which is good. But I hadn't gotten much of an update on my condition until now.

You're good. I played and replayed the words over and over in my mind, savouring the unspoken sound, slowly trying to wrap my head around what had just been said. Only two little words, yet a world of difference.

But still, I had a dozen questions that needed answering.

"I'm good!" I pronounced, still half in amazement. "But what does that mean? How good am I? Am I back to 100%?"

"There will be a recovery period," the doctor said. "But after that, you should be able to do anything a healthy person of your age and fitness level could do. Your heart is completely normal now.

The surgery was a success."

In that moment, I was more than good. I was fantastic. Tears started to roll down my cheeks. My dad was there to see me, and I held his hand. I just lay there and cried tears of relief and possibility.

I've always hated the connotations people have with the word 'surgery'. As soon as they hear that word, the same old questions emerge: "I heard you had surgery, is everything OK? Do you need any help? What's wrong with you?" Well, now there was nothing wrong with me. I was *good*.

I started training in earnest as soon as they let me out of the hospital. I had a triathlon to run, and nothing was going to stop me now. I was already stronger mentally than I'd ever been before in my life, and I was determined to make my body catch up.

I ran, swam, and biked further and faster than I'd ever done before. With nothing holding me back, I was free to break through my limits, even the limits I set for myself. Over the next seven weeks, I worked myself into the best shape of my life — better than when I competed in gymnastics, better than when I wrestled and played football, better than when I was in the prime of my youth.

With a whole lot of hard work and determination, I forged myself into a brand-new person.

No, not a new person. I was who I had always been, who I always knew I could be.

One of the biggest changes I made that pushed my fitness to a whole new level was with my diet. Before SVT, I tried to eat healthily, but I still had cheat days. I'm a bit ashamed to admit it now, but sometimes I felt like I was too busy to eat home-cooked food, so I'd grab a Big Mac on the way to work. I figured it was no big deal. I was still fitter than a lot of guys my age, so why worry about it? Then, during the darkest days of my SVT, insomniac nightmare, I wasn't caring enough about what I was eating. When you haven't slept for three days and you're on the verge of a mental collapse, a healthy diet isn't the first thing that pops into your head. But maybe it should be.

What I've learned since then, and what I'm trying to pass on to you, is that everything works in harmony. There is a balance to life, and when one dimension of your life is out of tune, the rest suffers along with it.

Sometimes, the problems you're facing can seem overwhelming, like some never-ending flight of stairs. I know I felt that way when I got diagnosed with SVT. Suddenly there is just this impossible scenario in front of you and you don't even know where to start.

Well, I'm here to tell you where to start: you start at the beginning.

You're not going to change overnight. I didn't change overnight.

That's not how it works, no matter how much you might wish it was. No, you start with one thing. For me, that was putting my trust in a power greater than myself. A step. Then I changed my way of thinking through cognitive thought. Another step. Sleep hygiene, exercise, diet: step, step, step.

Soon enough you're racing by; your steps thundering, getting quicker and quicker until you're running up that endless flight of stairs, only it doesn't look so endless any more. Now you can see the top, and you step, step, step, step, step until you're there. You put one foot in front of the other until you've reached the summit and can survey your surroundings from on high.

Remember, it doesn't matter where you start, as long as you start.

Take diet for example. I knew a bit about eating healthily — I was a gymnastics coach after all — but I was no nutritionist. If I were to jump off the deep end and try to fix my diet all in one fell swoop, I would have been overwhelmed. It would have been like the dramatic New Year's resolution: too much too fast.

Instead, I started small. I already knew from my research into sleep that you shouldn't eat before bed, so I cut out all snacking after ten p.m. From there, I cut it back to nine, then eight. A step within a step, but it got me started.

From there, I started making other changes in my diet, some small and some large. Here are a few of the tips and tricks I learned throughout my journey, which I later supplemented with intensive research into modern nutrition.

- Eating a balanced diet is essential for good health and wellbeing, with emphasis on *balanced.* You need a combination of protein, essential fats, complex carbohydrates, vitamins, and minerals to live, and we need a wide variety of foods to provide the right balance of nutrients.

- Digesting food takes time — about four hours to be specific. If you eat before going to bed, your mind might be resting but your body isn't. A good rule of thumb is to eat when the sun is out, not when the sun goes down.

- Reduce simple and refined sugars (e.g., white sugar, bread, pasta — if it's pure white, it's been bleached and is not the best for you)

- Balance your pH (the scale between acid and alkaline). You can do this by cutting back on things like excessive fatty meat, white sugar, and dairy and replacing them with greens, water, berries, and vegetables.

- Antioxidants are good! They help keep our immune systems strong and prevent us from getting sick. You can find them in common foods including blueberries and red peppers. Pro tip: most fruits or vegetables that are rich in antioxidants have darker, more vibrant skin.

- Aim to have half your meal be complex carbohydrates (vegetables), one quarter protein (fish, chicken, seafood or possibly lean meat or steak once or twice each week), one quarter good fats (avocado, olive oil, nuts).

- If all else fails, remember: pick, pull, kill. If you can't pick it off a branch, pull it out of the ground, or kill it, then think long and hard about whether or not this is something you should eat.

Nutrition can seem like a massively complicated topic. Am I getting enough of this vitamin/mineral? Is that carbohydrate simple or complex? Am I hitting all my macros? What even is an antioxidant? It can be intimidating stuff. So how should you approach nutrition? One step at a time.

For me, the simplest question of all reveals the most profound answer: how did we live before? Before fast food and frozen breakfasts, even before farming and agriculture. We gathered what was around us and we hunted what we could. Today, we've lost touch with those origins, with the way we're designed to operate.

Now, obviously, I'm not suggesting we go back to the Stone Age. Modern science and technology have produced some of the greatest wonders in human history. But why couldn't we learn from the way we lived before all these unnatural things we take for granted? We were meant to be omnivores, eating a variety of foods all around us, often walking upwards of ten kilometers a day in search of food.

Today, we're not functioning the way we're meant to function. We've lost touch with our past and it's hurting our present.

Now we sit on our couches and order food delivered to us with our cell phones. And people wonder why obesity and disease remain such vital concerns.

The connection with such a distant past might seem impossible to restore. I admit, it's difficult, but it is possible. You just have to go one step at a time. The same goes for health and exercise.

Sometimes, all it takes is that first step to get you moving on a path you could never have anticipated, whether that be running a triathlon or reinventing your diet.

And who knows, maybe the first step in your journey is to read this book.

Maybe this is just the first step in uncovering just how good you could be.

Failure and deprivation are the best educators and purifiers.

— *Albert Einstein*

CHAPTER ELEVEN
Who Taught You How to Think?

"So, what are you going to do now?"

I hadn't seen Suzanne in nearly a month, not since before my surgery. In that time, I felt like I'd become a new man. The cognitive thought principles she taught me, including oppositional thinking, had transformed the way I saw the world, and the surgery had done the same for my heart. I can't express how much my life had changed since the day I met her at the hospital at the end of the most exhausting seventy-two hours of my life.

Still, she got straight to the point, like no time at all had passed since our last meeting.

"Well, I was thinking about maybe doing a triathlon actually," I said. "I've been doing a lot of swimming and biking lately, so I figured I'd give it a shot."

"You're not going to do a triathlon," she said with a sureness that caught me off guard. I opened my mouth to object, but I was still trying to process what she had said.

"'Maybe I'll do a triathlon'; 'I figured why not'… listen to yourself, Aaron. What have we been working on these past few months?"

"Cognitive thought. Oppositional thinking mostly."

"And when you're practicing cognitive thought, trying to become more aware of your own thoughts and catch any negative ones before they cause problems, is there room for 'maybes'? When you're attempting to think in an oppositional way, do you say to yourself 'I guess I'm probably not afraid of SVT'? No, you have to be more confident. *I'm not, I repeat not, afraid of SVT. I'm not afraid to die. I'm healthy, I'm happy, I'm going to succeed in whatever I put my mind to.*"

I nodded attentively, but as I listened to Suzanne, another question came to mind.

"You're right. One hundred percent right. Hesitation is a killer — I've seen it thousands of times in gymnastics. A girl hesitates or she's not confident in her ability and that's what ruins her routine. But once I've gotten that confidence, once I have a crystal-clear picture in my mind of what I want to do, what then? Cognitive thought and oppositional thinking can't take me to where I need to go."

"Not by themselves," she said. "Remember, cognitive thought is like the ninja, dealing with bad thoughts as soon as they emerge. Then you have oppositional thinking to replace those thoughts with more positive, productive ones. But there's a lot more you have to do to achieve a complete mental balance. The next step, once you've identified a clear goal, is neuro-linguistic programming."

"Huh?" This was starting to sound like a high-school-English vocabulary quiz.

"You can call it NLP for short," she said.

"Ok, that's helpful… but I'm still not really following. What exactly is NLP?" I asked

"That's a bit of a complicated question. I'll try to explain using an analogy. Imagine that a man is riding a horse along a cobblestone path towards a castle. Can you picture it?"

"Sure."

"The man rides his horse down the path for a long while, then he comes to a river that he has to cross. Fortunately for him, there's an old, well-traveled bridge over the river. He starts to cross, but he notices that the stones that form the bridge are beginning to crumble. Suddenly, the bridge collapses, leaving the rider stranded on the wrong side of the river with seemingly no way to cross."

"All right, so how does this relate to neuro-whatever, NLP?"

"Consider this: In the story, the man wants something. He wants to reach the castle. He's just like the conscious mind, which sets a goal and tries to achieve it. The horse, the thing that he controls to try and reach his goal, is the subconscious mind. Like a horse, the subconscious mind doesn't have the inclination or the strength of will to accomplish much of anything — it needs to be driven, or ridden, by the conscious mind. Are you following me so far?"

"Rider equals conscious, horse equals subconscious. So, I guess that means the castle represents whatever your goal is."

"Exactly. And the path that the rider, the conscious mind, forces the horse, the subconscious mind, to follow is thought. Thought is the path, and that's the key to the whole image because the pathway breaks down. The rider follows the path as far as he can, just like our conscious minds try to follow the psychological paths that are most familiar to us. But in the story, the path breaks down, and therein lies the problem. What do we do when we want something really badly, but we can't think of any way to accomplish it? What happens when our paths of thought, our neurolinguistic bridges, break down or simply don't work for us?

"It happens every day," she continued. "We want something, but we don't know how to get it. The paths are broken — they don't work. So, what do we do? We create new paths. That's NLP.

"I'll get into the nitty-gritty details of NLP in another session, but first, I want to return to the analogy. Remember that the rider notices that the bridge is broken before he tries to cross it fully. That recognition is the first step we have to take if we're going to start practicing NLP. We have to recognize when a thought or a path isn't working and stop following it. Once we recognize that a thought is not working, we need to create new ways of thinking, new paths.

"In order to completely restructure our way of thinking, we need to alter the scripts that our minds follow. Doing that requires time and, perhaps most importantly, expertise. You can't just say to yourself one day, 'now I'm going to rewrite all the pathways of my brain'. Not possible. If you've conditioned yourself to a certain way of thinking, if you've only ever taken that one broken bridge for the past month, year, your entire life, then it's going to be hard to change. It can be almost impossible to do so by yourself. To overcome the temptation to fall into the same old, broken pathway that you've unconsciously followed hundreds, thousands, or even tens of thousands of times.

"Creating a new pathway is never easy. It's not going to be a nice, smooth, paved road. You're going off the beaten track, navigating through the tall grass where you haven't travelled before, and you're going to encounter bumps along the way. Even if your conscious mind, the rider, wants to go through these new paths, your subconscious mind, the horse, has no idea what's going on. It just wants to follow the same old ways that it's used to. A horse can be a stubborn animal, as can our subconscious. But it's our job, as the riders of our lives, to take charge.

"The first time you take a new path is going to be the hardest. However, the more you take the new path, the better or the healthier path, the easier it will get. The tangled woods and rough terrain will be cleared away, the path itself will become smooth and easy to travel.

And what will happen to the old, ineffective path? It will grow over with the long grass, become a path not easy to go down until only the positive path remains.

"That's how our minds work. If we tell ourselves something enough times, then we start to believe it. For example, you might say to yourself, 'I hate walking. My doctor told me I should walk more, but I just can't stand it'. A lot of people might assume that there's nothing you could do about that. They'd be wrong. If you tell yourself every day, 'I love walking' then guess what? Sooner or later, your subconscious mind will take a hint and realize that it likes to walk too.

"If you only take one thing away from this session, let it be this: you can achieve anything you want in life — anything at all — through the power of your mind. I know, I know, it sounds too good to be true. It can't be that simple. Well, I'm here telling you right now that it is. That nagging doubt, that constant unspoken fear, they don't need to exist. Some people never have those fears or doubts. If you rearrange your thinking, you can live a life of complete certainty, free from 'maybe' and 'I guess so'."

I trained every day from then on, only I wasn't just training my body — I was training my mind like I never had before. Sure, I had been practicing cognitive thought since before my surgery, but this was different. With a clear goal in mind, I was able to train in a structured manner. For every hour I put in at the gym or on the bike I must have spent just as long working on creating new thoughts and pathways.

As I put the reps in during my physical exercise, I could feel the strength returning to my muscles.

What shocked me even more, though, was how much disuse had affected my mind. It was like Suzanne had said, I'd been utterly reliant on a handful of old, battered, ineffective neurological pathways. If six months of physical inactivity had somewhat altered my bodily health, then several decades of faulty thinking had severely altered my neurological health. I had to rewrite not just a few bad thoughts or self-destructive pathways, I had to create a whole new way of seeing the world.

The process was long. At times, it felt like I was lost in the woods with no clue which way to go, but eventually, through careful coaching and hard work, it all started to click. In a sense, the experience was a bit like gymnastics, minus the trophy at the end. In the end, though, I got a far greater reward than I had ever received from gymnastics. I received the gift of a new life and freedom from the toxic thoughts that had gradually become normal to me.

At the same time, I started approaching a few other strategies and techniques to improve both my physical and mental health. One, in particular, bears mentioning, as it worked in tandem with the cognitive thought and NLP to reinvigorate my life. I'm talking about meditation.

I first began to meditate in the period leading up to my surgery as a way to deal with my insomnia. After more or less resolving my sleep issues, I continued the practice, though at first, I wasn't sure that meditation was overly helpful. I tried a few different techniques, most of which just involved some simple breathing exercises and visualization, and while I'm sure they didn't hurt, it wasn't until I discovered Transcendental Meditation that I noticed a huge change.

The type of meditation I learned to practice was the same one that Jerry Seinfeld, Ellen DeGeneres and some other well-known personalities practice. And it really works. Now, I'm no doctor nor do I pretend to be, but even an ordinary guy like me can see the results. Countless studies have shown that Transcendental Meditation is actually as effective as medicine at treating insomnia and PTSD. After my successful surgery, I continued to meditate, and the results were remarkable! Together with a host of other strategies and techniques, meditation helped restore balance to my life.

The key to it all was goal setting. I wanted to become the best version of myself I could possibly be. With such an abstract goal, how can we motivate ourselves to achieve anything? By setting a concrete, actualized goal like completing a triathlon.

Step by step, daily goal by daily goal, I progressed, I worked the steps and sub-steps of my plan. I was building towards something special, and I knew there was nothing that could stand in my way.

As the day of the triathlon crept closer, I was training harder than ever. In my mind, I had the all-clear from the doctors, so why not see how far I could push myself?

So, I did — I pushed and pushed until my body started pushing back.

It started as just a nagging feeling, a lack of energy, almost like I hadn't gotten a good night's sleep the night before. It was easy enough to just chalk it up to the training itself. Who doesn't feel a bit tired after training for a triathlon five days a week? So, I carried on without a second thought. I was good; the doctors had said so themselves.

Only, I wasn't feeling so good. In fact, I was feeling kind of like shit. When I ran, my legs quaked like Jell-O; when I swam, my arms dragged like anchors. Each day, just getting out of bed became more of a chore. I wasn't just tired after a workout; I was tired all the time. It was like all my hard work was slipping through my fingers and I wasn't sure what to do about it.

In my stubbornness, I stayed the course, training like mad and pushing my concerns to the side. Old habits die hard.

After putting in so much work to improve my health, I felt like I'd gone back to square one. I was running on fumes, and worse still, the fatigue was starting to affect my sleep. It wasn't as bad as before, thank God, but I was still struggling to get to sleep, sometimes tossing and turning for hours before finally settling down.

It sounds contradictory, and I suppose in a sense it is — being so tired that you can't sleep — but this wasn't a normal kind of fatigue. I was being drained of life, slowly but surely, and I didn't know why.

Except, in the back of my mind, I had a suspicion. In a dark corner I thought I'd gotten rid of months ago, a small voice whispered what I'd always been afraid of: what if the surgery hadn't worked?

No, the doctor said it worked. I was fine. He'd said so. After six months of waiting, all the doctor's appointments, three different hospitals, a specialist surgeon. I was fine.

But doctors make mistakes. It happens every day. Surgeries have complications. What if they missed something? The chances were slim, almost marginal, one in thousands. But what if I was the one? Maybe there was a problem. Maybe it was still there, maybe I still had…

No, no, no, it was over. I was healthy. There was no way I still had SVT. Supraventricular tachycardia, what would I give to never hear those damn words again. It was over. I never needed to think about it again. I was healthy. I was sleeping right, eating right, exercising. Could I do all that if I still had SVT?

Could I do it now, though? The past few weeks had been miserable. Something was wrong.

My head was spinning, caught between the calming voice of reason and an old, resurrected seed of doubt:

Something is wrong.
You're good. *You're sick.*
It's over.
It's never over.
I'm going to run a triathlon. *What about your heart?*
I'm going to run a triathlon.
What about the surgery?
I'm not afraid.
I'm petrified.

I had to know. I'd hoped to run a triathlon in two months, but that plan was torn to shreds. Now I just wanted to know what was going on. If there was something wrong with me, I had to figure out what it was as soon as possible. I couldn't live with the uncertainty.

I visited the doctor and been given the prognosis about my growing weakness, which I feared might stem from complications from the surgery or even a relapse of SVT. Thankfully, the doctor put all my worries to bed. He assured me that what I was suffering from wasn't related to SVT at all. I was suffering from adrenal fatigue, probably brought on by excessive exercise following my surgery so closely.

In retrospect, it seems obvious — don't train like a madman immediately after having heart surgery — but I did. Fortunately, the prescription was simple and 100% effective: just rest.

I had to cancel my plans to run a triathlon that year, but other than that, I suffered no lasting effects from the adrenal fatigue apart from a slightly bruised ego. I'd done it again, pushed myself too hard, too fast. I was a touch embarrassed and annoyed with myself, but otherwise, the doctors had been right the first time: I was good.

I took a few months off from training strenuously and planned to run the same triathlon the following year.

I had been dealing with adrenal fatigue and post-traumatic stress disorder.

For people with PTSD, triggers can lurk in even the most common places. Memories of the traumatic event can intrude into your mind whenever you're reminded of the traumatic event. Now imagine that your traumatic experience stems from your own heartbeat. That can be pretty hard to avoid, especially when you live an active lifestyle.

In retrospect, I had all the typical symptoms of PTSD immediately after my first major attack. I kept reliving the experience, time and time again; I avoided talking about my trauma whenever I could; my attitude changed completely, taking on an incredibly dark, negative outlook; even my physical health suffered, including my sleep pattern. If you find yourself experiencing any of those symptoms, especially if you've recently gone through a traumatic event, look into professional help and talk to someone about how you're feeling.

As I'm sure it has become abundantly clear throughout this book, I can be stubborn to a fault. I couldn't see the symptoms that were right in front of my face. Then, after the surgery, I thought I was all better. I was healthy, happy, and ready to move on with my life. But even though I had discovered something to believe in, even though I improved my mental health, even though I'd been practicing cognitive thought, even though I'd balanced my diet and exercised regularly, I wasn't 'cured'.

There is no cure, no one thing I can tell you that will instantly solve your problems. All I can say is that we are all on a journey, one with bumps and roadblocks along the way but also incredible joys that make it all worthwhile. One day, perhaps, I will become the person I was always capable of becoming. I know I'm far closer today than I was before my SVT diagnosis. But there is still work to do every single day.

For my PTSD, I had to face my problems head-on. That meant a lot more work on my mental health. It meant accepting that I would always have those memories — they are a part of me now, that's just how it is.

CHAPTER TWELVE
Survive and Thrive

It was a cool day, all things considered. Late August usually retains the warmth of the heart of summer, but on that day, I could feel a brisk Georgia breeze blowing in. Not that it was unpleasant: the opposite, in fact. The cool wind felt refreshing as I readied myself for what was to come.

Today was the day I'd been waiting for. Today I would have an answer to all the questions I'd been asking. As I sat in the early morning darkness, waiting, I thought of all the people who had brought me to that point. I recalled all the difficulties I'd gone through to get here, all the hard work, the sleepless nights — all of it.

It all came down to a moment, and the moment was here.

I slipped into the early morning water and prepared to test myself.

There were about one hundred of us assembled, bobbing in the near darkness.

As I looked from face to face, I couldn't help but wonder what had brought them here. There were people older and younger than me. Some were tall, others short.

Each had a story, one I would never know, but I could certainly imagine. Perhaps some had gone through illnesses of their own. Some might have lost a loved one, others might have lost a job. Maybe others had PTSD, or anxiety, or insomnia, or even SVT.

As we gathered, preparing to embark on a grueling race, I was struck by how far I had come since Trois-Rivières. We all have a burden to bear, but in the end, we are masters of our own destinies.

I could have given up a long time ago. I could have lost hope or accepted that it was impossible to complete a triathlon with a heart defect. But I didn't — none of us did. Instead, we were gathered to push ourselves.

As the moment drew closer, my focus narrowed. I'd been using everything I've come to rely on in my search for recovery and the pursuit of something bigger. My sleep was on point. Meditation had left me calm. My diet had carved out a chiselled body. Muscles and lungs were at the ready from the fitness regime I had been following. My mind wouldn't let a negative idea in. I was a cognitive instrument pumping out only the most positive of thoughts.

The starter's pistol pierced the silent dawn and I plunged beneath the surface of the dark cool water and pushed forward towards my fate. As the race unfolded, I embraced my new self and enjoyed every single second. From the swim, through the transition, onto my bike pushing up hills and flying down winding descents at breakneck speeds.

Last came the run, I was certain that I had passed many of my fellow triathletes that beautiful Georgia morning and that I hadn't been passed by anyone who looked remotely close to my age. I'd be damned if I was going to let that happen now. As I came to the finishing straight, the large crowd that lined each side came clearly into view. I heard the announcer call out, "Here comes Aaron Brokenshire, all the way from Ontario, Canada! Our first competitor in the men's 45-plus division so far today! Let's give him a warm Georgia welcome to the finish line!"

As I passed over the finish line everything went silent. It was just me and the sun on my face, embracing me like a warm hug. I slowed to a walk and kept on going, past the crowd, beyond the last resonance of any encouragement and acclaim. Past everyone, down the hill, wading into the still water where I began the day. No one was there. No one at all. Overcome with emotion I sank down into the cool water and let it all come out. The full weight of this frenzied, torturous and exhausting journey hitting me and leaving me all at once.

I had made it. I had survived. And then, I had thrived.

From an ambulance ride through insomnia to calling out for help or death, to lying on the operating table, to this... to winning a triathlon. Wow! We are capable of so much. Each and everyone one of us, we can be amazing athletes, fathers, mothers, teachers, students, entrepreneurs, fitness enthusiasts, sons and daughters. We can be and do anything we want when we set our full intention at it. All you have to do is start by asking yourself: "How Good Could You Be?"

Epilogue
Bulls and Turtles

Context changes everything.

A few months later, we found ourselves basking in the Florida sunshine. At the time, I didn't think much of it. I'd been fortunate enough to make dozens of trips to Florida in my life, from the annual vacations when I was a kid to my renewed love affair with the region after my trips there with Angela. I'd even come to foresee certain things on those trips: lots of sunshine, a relaxing atmosphere, and quality time with family. This time, though, on what I thought was just a normal family vacation, I experienced something new.

The night before, we'd checked into Cheeca Lodge in the village of Islamorada in the Florida Keys. Angela and I had been to the Keys many times since we were married there. After the kids were born, it became the go-to destination for our nearly annual family trips. Although this wasn't our first visit, you wouldn't have known it from Ava and Gavin's excitement. They were still too young to have a worry in the world.

After spending the night at the lodge, we had a busy day planned. We started our morning by heading down to the beach for a quick swim. As the gentle waves

187

rolled over the white pebbly beach, lapping warm water on our feet before returning to the vast, perfectly clear ocean, I could feel all the tension leave my body, washing away any stress I might have brought with me from back home. Even so, the main event was still to come.

Before setting out for the beach, I called ahead and scheduled a scuba dive with a local dive operator. Although I don't get a chance to indulge in it as often as some other hobbies, scuba diving has been a passion for years, one that I've grown to appreciate even more as I've gotten older. Nothing can match the freedom you get and the incredible alien worlds you see diving below the surface.

At that point, the kids were still a bit too young to be scuba diving, so in the afternoon, Angela and the kids headed back to the pool while I set out in the dive boat headed for a local reef. We planned to meet up again in the afternoon, but I was looking forward to taking some alone time.

When we got to the reef, the water was almost completely still and perfectly clear — the sort of water where you felt you could almost see all the way to the bottom. I was with just a handful of other divers, including the divemaster, the person in charge of supervising the dive and making sure nobody does anything dangerous. He gave us our instructions and we prepared to dive.

I was second into the water, followed shortly by four more divers and the divemaster himself. Immediately, we made our way to the reef, looking for the array of life one inevitably discovers clustered around those magnificent structures. This wasn't my first reef dive, and I was prepared for the varieties of colourful fish and bright coral structures. But I wasn't prepared for what came next.

Directly in front of me, not more than ten feet away, an enormous sea turtle appeared from seemingly nowhere. Its shell alone must have been three feet across, but it moved with the gracefulness of a ballerina, its four large flippers propelling it effortlessly through the water. Slowly, delicately, it headed in my direction, singling me out and for a moment, time seemed to stop. I knew that the other divers were behind me, but in that instant, I was completely alone. They existed in another world, somewhere as far from me as Waterloo was from Florida.

The mammoth turtle stopped moving its flippers and began to just float, moving neither closer nor further. It was so close that I could have reached out my hand and touched it, but I dared not disrupt the perfect moment. We remained transfixed on each other, I admired the intricate pattern of its shell and the powerful beak that tipped the broad head. It was an incredible creature, one that to this day I can recall with almost photographic detail.

At last, I stretched out my hand and placed it on the turtle's shell. Neither it nor I moved for what seemed like an eternity, though I know the whole scene couldn't have lasted longer than a minute. But even timeless moments must eventually come to an end, and with a flick of its golden flippers, it swam away. Ducking its head under my arm, it slipped underneath me, brushing its shell along my stomach as it passed.

I've been on many dives since then, but I've never had another experience like that. I've been diving amongst sharks. I've seen countless species of fish, but I've never seen or experienced anything remotely close to that day.

In the years that followed, I often thought of that turtle, the encounter was some incredibly good luck. After the surgery, however, I started to see it in a different light. I started to see it for the sign it was.

Ever since I started my own business, I'd used a charging bull as part of the branding. I had it on my business cards, I put it everywhere. Remember, I was the charging bull. I was full of fire and hunger. That was who I was.

In the aftermath of my SVT diagnosis, I wasn't so sure about that any more. Who I was, had changed. I wasn't the man I used to be. The bull was gone, although I wasn't quite sure what was left to take its place. Then, when I started to think back to that surreal moment with the sea turtle, everything just clicked.

I wasn't the bull any more — I was the turtle.

I wanted to go slower through life. I wanted to take it all in and appreciate the smaller things in life. I wanted to live longer and healthier, not just faster and stronger. As I recovered from the surgery, I started to read many books about philosophy, which really helped put into perspective what's important in life. Why are we here? Is it just to make a lot of money and win as many competitions as possible? Maybe the young bull might have thought so, but the (hopefully) wise turtle knows otherwise.

With that realization, my entire understanding of success changed. I still wanted to improve myself, I was still passionate about seeing how good I could be, but my definition of 'good' wasn't the same. Success isn't just about your career, your money, or your accomplishments. It's not even all about your health, your happiness, or your family. Success is about balancing these focus points in your life and helping others.

Don't get me wrong, your career is important. Family is incredibly important. But there's more to success than any single factor. To be truly successful, I had to find a way to balance work, family, exercise, and countless other things. That's why this book is structured the way it is. The chapters are intended to give you a guideline for some of the important dimensions of your life, but they don't cover everything. Life is so much more complicated than that. Ultimately, it's up to you to take what you've learned from all my trials, failures, and successes and apply it in your own life. If you do that, if I was able to help you find some balance, conquer your fears and embrace the possibilities of the best version of yourself, then the aim of this book has been fulfilled.

Take these ideas, make them your own. Go out and see how good you can be!

Acknowledgements

In my own life, there have been countless people who helped me on my way and without whom I would not be here today.

My mother: my constant supporter. Without her kindness, generosity, and undying encouragement, I would never have had the courage to change careers midstream or face my condition day in and day out.

My father: my earliest role model and driver of my ambition. We haven't always had the smoothest relationship, but I owe him more than I could ever express. He taught me what it means to support a family and not to lose sight of where you come from.

My brother, Greg: my first friend, and one who's still always there if I need a hand. He's a pillar of calm reason and I'm truly grateful for his lead.

My friend, co-worker and best listener in the world: Sarah. Imagine someone actually witnessed this ordeal from start to finish. Was there at Elite Canada when I went down, was there at the gym every day since. Imagine listening to someone straight-up lose their mind for months and then regain it, all while never casting a judgement. Sarah, if it weren't for you being there every day to listen and support me, this story would have been very different. Thank you from the bottom of my heart. You are a wise soul and an amazing friend.

My coaching friends: Lawson, who was there for me during my first major attack, and Kelly, who was there for me during my last attack. Both are there for me unconditionally and that's rare these days.

My great peers and mentors: Elvira taught me more about gymnastics than most coaches will learn in a lifetime. Vladi, what more can I say about Vladi? One of the gentlest, most intelligent men I've ever known. He showed me it was possible to have it all.

My brilliant doctors and nurses: I know I complain about them sometimes, but I wouldn't be standing here without them. They literally saved my life.

Finally, my own family: Angela, the love of my life, the stable centre in a world full of chaos. There aren't enough words in the world to express how much she means to me. Ava and Gavin, my beautiful children, whose smiles light up my day no matter what. Those three above all are the reason I strive to be the best person I can be, to be the husband and father that they unquestionably deserve.

All of these people supported me through thick and thin, making possible everything I have talked about in this book. The gratitude I feel towards them is something that can never be tarnished. It runs through my veins, invigorating me, pushing me to new heights. It courses through my newly healed heart. It is the lifeblood of my accomplishments, the source of the balance I know today and that I hope you will know in the future.

Seminars and Workshops with Aaron Brokenshire, Author and Public Speaker

Aaron Brokenshire is one of North America's most energetic, passionate and relatable speakers. His experience and insight on adversity, grit, oppositional thinking and energy have made him a standout choice for corporations, wellness-retreat organizers, and convention coordinators. Aaron's concepts will inspire you and yours to confront your fears, move beyond pain and lay the blueprint to becoming your highest functioning selves.

Contact us today to start planning your customized experience designed to motivate and propel your people towards becoming their highest functioning selves.

To book Aaron or for further inquiries please visit advenshire.com